EmotiConversations

EmotiConversations

Working through Our Deepest Places

John Elton Pletcher
Holly Hall-Pletcher

Foreword by Bill Peel

RESOURCE *Publications* · Eugene, Oregon

EMOTICONVERSATIONS
Working through Our Deepest Places

Copyright © 2016 John Elton Pletcher and Holly Hall-Pletcher. All rights reserved. Except for brief quotations in critical publications or reviews, no part of this book may be reproduced in any manner without prior written permission from the publisher. Write: Permissions, Wipf and Stock Publishers, 199 W. 8th Ave., Suite 3, Eugene, OR 97401.

Resource Publications
An Imprint of Wipf and Stock Publishers
199 W. 8th Ave., Suite 3
Eugene, OR 97401

www.wipfandstock.com

PAPERBACK ISBN: 978-1-4982-8250-5
HARDCOVER ISBN: 978-1-4982-8252-9

Manufactured in the U.S.A.

Scripture taken from the Common English Bible®, CEB® Copyright © 2010, 2011 by Common English Bible.™ Used by permission. All rights reserved worldwide. The "CEB" and "Common English Bible" trademarks are registered in the United States Patent and Trademark Office by Common English Bible. Use of either trademark requires the permission of Common English Bible.

Scripture quotations marked (ESV) are from The Holy Bible, English Standard Version® (ESV®), copyright © 2001 by Crossway, a publishing ministry of Good News Publishers. Used by permission. All rights reserved. Scripture quotations taken from the New American Standard Bible®, Copyright © 1960, 1962, 1963, 1968, 1971, 1972, 1973, 1975, 1977, 1995 by The Lockman Foundation Used by permission. (www.Lockman.org)
Scripture taken from the Holy Bible, NEW INTERNATIONAL VERSION®. Copyright © 1973, 1978, 1984, 2011 by Biblica, Inc. All rights reserved worldwide. Used by permission.

Scripture quotations marked NLT are taken from the *Holy Bible*, New Living Translation, copyright © 1996, 2004. Used by permission of Tyndale House Publishers, Inc., Carol Stream, Illinois 60188. All rights reserved.

For Nanc', Jarod, Joel, and Josiah

You supply me with joy-filled days and brighter ways of handling my own deep places. God's never-give-up love and beautiful blessings constantly smile through the four of you toward others—including my own soul.—JEP

For Betsy, Dan, John, Nancy, and all the "grands"

Thank you for filling my days with your love and care. You have walked so patiently with me throughout my life's journey and shared times of joy and laughter, as well as seasons of tears and great sorrow. I love you all very much and am so richly blessed to have such a wonderful family. Also, for my co-grandmother and dear friend, Bev McBride, who is currently traveling her own Naomi journey. May our God of all grace always sustain you and bring you great comfort and peace.—HHP

The world is indeed full of peril, and in it there are many dark places; but still there is much that is fair, and though in all lands love is now mingled with grief, it grows perhaps the greater.

—J.R.R. TOLKIEN

Contents

Foreword by Bill Peel | ix
Introduction—Your Emotions at Work | xiii

ONE   Commotion on the Field | 1
TWO   Dark 'n Stormy | 15
THREE   Oh, Good Grief! | 32
FOUR   Flourishing in a Financial Crunch | 49
FIVE   Hard 'n Hearty Work | 65
SIX   Romantic Roller Coasters | 91
SEVEN   Bitter to Better—Really? | 110
EIGHT   Redemption's Long-Range Reach | 126

Afterword & Acknowledgements | 149
About the Authors | 155
Bibliography | 157

Foreword

By sheer force of time and focus, our workplaces have an overwhelmingly strong, shaping influence on our hearts and character. Our work, whether we are closing a sale, plowing a field, teaching a class, or managing a household, plays an oft-unanticipated role in our spiritual growth. We learn truth at church and in personal and group Bible studies, but the workplace is most often where godly character is molded, tried, and tested. It is there that the transforming power of the gospel can make truth real to us in everyday experiences of joy and pain, peace and conflict, victory and defeat, prosperity and scarcity—and make us more like Jesus.

However, when the most powerful, life-altering, culture-changing force in the world—the gospel of Jesus Christ—is left behind, as it frequently is when we enter our workplaces, secular values will inevitably mold the hearts of faithful churchgoers. Cultural values and practices prevalent in our world today can whittle away at the thin influence of a few moments of worship on Sunday. Caught in the pull between the everyday realities of the workplace and the revelation of our identity in Christ, commitments and good intentions made during Sunday worship can evaporate quickly under the heat of daily pressure and competition.

According to sociologist James Davison Hunter, we are all being spiritually formed; the question is, by what.

> The problem for Christians—to restate the broader issue once more—is not that their faith is weak, or inadequate. ... while they have faith, *they have also been formed by the larger post-Christian culture,* a culture whose habits of life less and less resemble anything like the vision of

Foreword

human flourishing provided by the life of Christ and the witness of scripture.[1]

This presents both a serious challenge and an opportunity for both Christians and their leaders charged with making disciples. Fortunately, a growing number of influencers are beginning to take this seriously. Pastor John Pletcher is one. I first met John Pletcher through his book, *Henry's Glory*, a creative account of a biblical theology of work conveyed in a fiction format. Later, I had the privilege of speaking at the church he pastors in Pennsylvania and seeing firsthand one church's commitment to discipling people for their workplaces.

In *EmotiConversations*, John has teamed with his mother and educator, Holly Hall-Pletcher, to explain how Christians can view their work and the various emotions work evokes as significant opportunities for spiritual formation. According to the Pletchers, the emotions we feel give us a real-time indication of what is going on in our hearts that can help us respond intentionally as Christ-followers. On the other hand, when ignored or mishandled, emotions too often lead to responses more characteristic of our non-Christian coworkers than reflective of Jesus' character, the very character we are charged to display to them.

Using the biblical story of Ruth as a framework, *EmotiConversations* is filled with practical insight, personal examples, and biblical wisdom. If you have thought of the Book of Ruth as primarily addressing family life and romance, think again. Though it certainly has relevance to these areas of life, as you will see, it is a book about economics and business relationships as much as anything else. After reading the following pages and gleaning wisdom from Ruth, Naomi, and Boaz, you will recognize just how important their story can be for your work. After all, Jesus' ancestors, Ruth and Boaz, met in the workplace. Moreover, following their story, you will come away with a significant grasp of the fact that God is at work—in us, through us, and alongside us—as we do our work. That reality will shape the way we do our work, how

---

1. Hunter, *To Change the World*, 227.

Foreword

we face the circumstances in our work, and how we respond to the various emotions we experience as Christ is formed in us.

Bill Peel, ThM, DMin

Center for Faith & Work
at LeTourneau University
Dallas, Texas

INTRODUCTION

Your Emotions at Work

Soaked in the delectable smell of buttery popcorn, we laughed uproariously and cried profusely—all in the same ninety minutes. From young to old, moviegoers were both wildly entertained and winsomely educated by Disney-PIXAR's *INSIDE OUT*. Creatively set in the mind of a vivacious middle school girl, five personified emotions—Joy, Sadness, Fear, Anger, and Disgust—work hard to lead Riley as she moves with her parents to San Francisco. The blockbuster masterfully delivers a brilliantly captivating story while simultaneously educating audiences in how human emotions are constantly working—from the inside out—in all we think, feel, do, and say.

We readily resonate with such animated, comedic drama. Emotional dynamics are at work in kids of all ages. Deep in our daily selves, our souls face a grand mix of life circumstances and accompanying emotions—fear, anger, joy, grief, despair, hope, and many more! And we experience these in every field of life—at the office, in the shop, with family and friends, in our neighborhoods—even while texting across our smartphones and messaging via social media.

Emotions are everywhere, and especially in our daily workplaces. Paul Stevens and Alvin Ung observe: "The workplace is a major arena for the battle of our souls. We spend many of our waking hours at work. We are besieged daily by hundreds of work-related thoughts and decisions that lead to good or evil."[1] In the pages to come, we wrestle with this big question: What if we begin to consciously view our workplace emotions as gigantic

---

1. Stevens and Ung, *Taking Your Soul to Work*, 11.

opportunities for spiritual formation as well as positive influence in the lives of others?

Up against our own inside-out challenges, we regularly stuff emotions, run far away, or distance ourselves from other people in our attempts to "go it alone." We are all tested with how to respond to the full mix—frustrations, temptations, and triumphant gladness—the ebb and flow continually inside each of us. What if we dare to "face in" and actually let God use our emotions to grow us, change us, and transform us into the image of Christ—for the sake of others?

Across this eight-chapter journey, you are in for a great adventure of courageous conversations, deeper development, and positive impact, both in your own spiritual formation and in potential Christ-like blessing for coworkers, clients, neighbors, and family. Though this book is thoroughly empowering when worked through solo, it will be best experienced as you read and discuss it with your team, in a small group of friends, or with your book club over coffee. You will grasp vital points of spiritual-emotional wisdom, and you have the opportunity at each chapter's wrap-up to contemplate deeper questions for next-level development.

When sharing personalized stories and reflections, we have identified who is sharing by parenthetical statement of our initials (JEP or HHP). We have prayed God's gracious blessing over these pages and your heart as you join the conversations. Across your journey, anticipate personal, spiritual-emotional development and an immense overflow of blessing to others.

John Elton Pletcher
Lancaster, PA

Holly Hall-Pletcher
Newark, OH

Fall 2015

CHAPTER ONE

Commotion on the Field

I will not say, do not weep,
for not all tears are an evil.
—J.R.R. TOLKIEN

Six to zip in the bottom of the third, the Mountville Pirates trudged back to the dugout. Dust scattered as the team of boys slapped their gloves on the ground in frustration and slumped back on the bench. Desperately behind, their deficit seemed staggering. Josiah (JEP's son, HHP's grandson) was nine years old and a baseball fanatic. He and his Pirate friends had worked hard all season and held a commanding record with just one previous loss all year. Here they were, semi-finals, the end-of-season tourney—everything was riding on this game. Now, their typically jolly faces wore dismal frowns. From the edges of a few boys' eyes, tears of anguish were leaking and streaking their tough-guy eyeblack. All seemed desperately lost.

Coaches (typically the players' dads) have their work cut out for them in such high-stakes games. Grown men battle their own emotions under pressure, and they are also tasked with trying to lift young athletes' attitudes, infuse fresh optimism, and otherwise inspire a rally. It's not just true for baseball players and coaches. Corporate executives, restaurant servers, single moms, high school principals, administrators of nonprofits, sales team leaders—people in every field—face the daily dilemma of juggling their emotions in the wake of seemingly loser circumstances.

EmotiConversations

Your board meeting is super-charged with tension. Caustic debate is layered so thick, you could slice the air. Everyone feels it. What do you do? Clam up? Get up and storm out? Speak up? Cut up in an attempt to lighten the room? Or step up in the dialog with winsome responses? Emotional choices are the big game changer.

It's been an ugly sales month (actually, a rotten *six* months, if you're honest). Several buddies invite you to join them at the pub on a Thursday evening, "just to take your mind off things." You think to yourself, "Could be dangerous, but what the hey—I could sure use a diversion." You know your own history, so you promise yourself you won't have more than two. Forty-five minutes later, the laughter is flowing uproariously, nicely matching the fine lager. You've already reached your limit. What do you do? Emotional choices are the big game changer.

The kids have been pushing all your buttons. They *are* good kids, and you love them like crazy, but this afternoon every conversation is a battle. They're squabbling. You can't seem to please them, no matter what you do or say. So far, you've kept your cool, repeatedly biting your tongue and telling yourself, "They're just kids and still growing up." Suddenly, the three-year-old leaps from the coffee table. Your Tiffany lamp goes flying—it's all unfolding in slow motion now—even the dog is fleeing the scene—CRASH! Hundreds of glass shards go flying across your oak floor. What instantaneously wells up and goes flying across your lips, and at what decibel level? Emotional choices are the big game changer.

How we feel about emotions—then and now

Historically, emotions have gotten a bad rap. At pivotal points across the centuries, hearty appreciation for growth in emotional understanding has proven to be seriously lacking. Emotions were positioned by many philosophers as negatively "hot" and seriously at odds with the sensibility of "cool" reason. Plato of Ancient Greece, ever a proponent of dichotomizing, envisioned the human soul like a chariot driver with two horses. One horse was on the right moving in the direction of the driver's fair and good reason.

But on the left side, a dark horse proved to be wild and reckless, spurred on by the driver's passion. Centuries later, René Descartes further fostered a dualistic view, associating the human mind with strong and healthy cognition. In contrast, the human body conveyed passions and spirits resulting in feelings and emotions. Such historic perspectives entrenched a dualism of mind/body and thinking/feeling.[1]

With such a distinct dichotomy promoted by key philosophers, emotions have been classically relegated to a lower value. In addition, emotions have raised their fair share of heated debate among scientists. Running in tandem with such dis-integrated ideology, much of the debate in neuroscience during the past two centuries has involved the issue of the body's role in emotional experiences. Researchers have asked and clashed over this question: Can there even be an emotional response without the body's involvement? Late 19th-century researcher William James worked to inextricably link the body with emotional reactions. In contrast, 20th-century researchers Walter Cannon and Philip Bard aimed to establish the subcortical location for emotion, thus downplaying the body's interplay with emotional reactions and relegating emotions to their own privatized, internal world in the neural processes. For several decades, Cannon and Bard's experimentation overshadowed James' emotions-body connections. However, more recent research has bolstered a reemergence of support for new variations of James' more integrated theory.[2]

> We readily recognize emotions at work throughout the complexity of our lives, but we seldom slow down to thoughtfully grapple with their actual nature.

Today, we readily recognize emotions at work throughout the complexity of our lives, but we seldom slow down to thoughtfully grapple with their actual nature. Across decades of research, experts have engaged in great debate on a quest for a precise definition. Elizabeth Johnston and Leah Olson shy away from supplying a final declaration, hedging "there is still no single answer to

---

1. Johnston and Olson, *The Feeling Brain*, xii-xiii.
2. Ibid., 5-10.

the question 'What is an emotion?' Most researchers now agree that emotional systems act to provide meaning and value to the information being processed; emotions tell us what we like and don't like, what is good for us and what is bad for us." Based on their own review and synthesis, Johnston and Olson supply an insightful conclusion: "All of the researchers we have studied share a conception of emotion/feeling as fundamentally assigning value to a stimuli and events. Organisms are continually bombarded by a wealth of information—from outside and inside the body and brain—and emotions provide a way of evaluating and prioritizing what to respond to."[3] Hence, our emotions deliver real-time evaluation and prioritization of the information coming our way, whether you're seated in a heated boardroom, at the pub wrestling your just-one-more demon, or standing in your own glass-strewn meltdown of rage mixed with tears.

Neel Burton joins the puzzlement over how to define emotions. Admitting a definition is not easy to state, he proceeds to distinguish emotions from humanity's typical traits, like moods, desires, perceptions, and beliefs. Burton comes closest to a declaration of emotion's meaning with this synopsis: "An emotion is above all a felt attitude or stance towards an object or class of object. This felt attitude is automatic and often unconscious, and is appropriate or justified if it reflects the relation between the object and subject, which itself is a function of context and values."[4]

An all-too-familiar emotional theater for our family has emerged while eating out. After we are seated and orders are placed, my (JEP) youngest son convinces the oldest to play him in tic-tac-toe. Josiah loves to play the game, but he is still learning the basics, strategy, and the important skill of distraction. Our oldest son, Jarod, still loves to play. He's shrewd and also ferociously competitive. Most of all, he does not believe in showing mercy or humoring a competitor. Jarod must always be Xs. He has been ruthlessly beating his mother for years. She obviously can handle losing, but when

---

3. Ibid., xi and 308-309.
4. Burton, *Heaven and Hell*, 14.

Jarod trounces Josiah, there is sudden weeping, wailing, and gnashing of teeth. Josiah either melts down or blows up.

Employing the above descriptors, Josiah's automatic emotions supply certain felt attitudes toward his big brother. Typically, these include dismay, anger, tears, and disgust. His general evaluation of Jarod is "BIG JERK!" His prioritization includes, "I'm done playing Jarod. I want to play Mom; she might let me win!" It's a very messy way to begin what was intended to be a nice family time over dinner out. More often these days, we just hide the placemats and crayons.

While experts struggle to precisely define emotions and some even fastidiously split hairs over the difference between emotions and feelings, we will employ the more popular descriptors and synonyms throughout this book. When we speak of emotions, we will be referring to how we commonly feel and how we react—both knee-jerk, gut reactions—as well as those responses that are more careful, thoughtful, and skillfully developed over time.

Why explore emotions?

Recent decades evidence burgeoning levels of research related to human emotion, including biological, psychological, and sociological studies. However, mucky misunderstandings still prevail, in spite of our obsession with talk shows and self-help literature. Most of us express personal passion to be healthy people who do healthy things, but ironically, we do not habitually *do* emotions in healthy ways.

I (HHP) threw my knitting project across the room with a vengeance. Immediately ashamed of my frustrated, angry outburst, I began to pray, asking God's forgiveness for such an ugly display of emotion. Seldom in my life could I remember throwing anything in a fit of temper. What caused such a shameful, emotional outburst?

Perhaps my explosion was due to the fact that I had just spent the better part of an hour listening to the pterodactyl screaming of my foster grandson, Stevie. Not quite two years old, this little guy seemed hotwired for at least one major temper tantrum each day. It was as if some unseen button was pushed, and then Stevie was stuck in the "on" position. I knew how I might have handled my own child, but foster children call for different care. None of the recommended practices seemed to work today. Only when his battery wore down would the terrible tantrum cease.

Exasperated, I went over and picked him up off the floor. Kicking and screaming, he fought me all the way. But at last he was deposited on a chair. "Blow your nose. Take a drink of water. Let Gram wash your face with this nice cool washrag." I gently put my arm around him and rubbed his trembling back. Stevie was a mess. His nose was running down his face. He was soaked with perspiration. His beautiful brown eyes were almost swollen shut. He began to take deep ragged breaths, and gradually the screaming subsided into hiccups. "Now are you ready to sit on Gram's lap?" I asked. He nodded. We changed his wet clothing and then went to sit in the big, soft chair. Stevie was totally worn out and fell asleep in my arms.

After I put Stevie down in his bed, I returned to the living room and picked up the lace shawl I was knitting. That's when I discovered the ugly mistake on the back. That's when my own terrible temper storm had occurred! As I began the tedious, many-rows process of "frogging" (Rip It! Rip It! Rip It!) to correct my knitting error, a Frank Sinatra song my mother sang to me as a child played in my head. "Just pick yourself up, dust yourself off, and start all over again." I pondered my anger. Stevie was not even two. I was sixty-five. I was a mature Christian woman. Certainly, I could have done better at managing my emotions.

Well-loved speaker Charles Swindoll has boldly reflected, "The Christian life is not a playground. It is a battleground."[5] I believe much of that battle has to do directly with emotions. Each day we must work to evaluate and express wisely our own emotions while striving to understand and communicate proper responses to the emotions of others. We enjoy discussing positive

---

5. Swindoll, *Insight for Living Daily Podcast: Traveling a Rough and Rugged Road Part 2*, aired July 23, 2015.

emotions such as love, joy, peace, and contentment. But let's face it. Emotions are like feet. We have them, and in all honesty they sometimes stink! I learned from my day with Stevie, we are never too young or too old to learn timely truths about communicating emotions.

> Workplace leaders typically express personal passion to be healthy people who do healthy things, but ironically, we do not habitually *do* emotions in healthy ways.

Throughout broad societal framework, both personal and familial structures remain abysmally dysfunctional—especially related to emotions. Hardly any of us are *normal* anymore, as if we are most noble when we foster the *fun* in dysfunctional. And too often, we just shrug. "*Que sera, sera*. Whatever will be, will be." Burton observes, "With the decline of religion and traditional social structures, our emotions, though maladapted to modern times, have come to assume an increasingly dominant role in our lives . . . Yet, remarkably, the emotions are utterly neglected by our system of education, leading to millions of mislived lives."[6] Oodles of intentional hours and dollars are spent pursuing diet, exercise, and cognitive success through higher education. Does it not seem equally appropriate for us to pursue this vital realm of our emotional health?

Sadly, such general malaise appears equally true in Christian communities, in spite of our best efforts through church services, classes for Bible study, well-intended counseling, support groups, and one-to-one discipleship. Why do we remain fixated on quick fixes, feel-good sound bites, and supposed growth through external behaviorism? For Christians—people whose hallmark focus has classically been all things soulful, internal, and spiritual—how is it that we glibly ignore more thoughtful engagement with this oh-so-vital arena of human emotions. Shouldn't we sincerely *dig deeper*—to explore, correlate, and otherwise apply healthy emotions in pursuit of personal spiritual development?

---

6. Burton, *Heaven and Hell*, ix.

EMOTICONVERSATIONS

What's your commotion?

So the two of us feel compelled to just admit it at the outset—we both have emotional issues. (It actually does feel good to own them, at least some of them.) Our family has walked through a feelings-charged decade of losses and enormous transitions in a tapestry of arenas. We have experienced a great deal of commotion and ugly fragmentation (more juicy details are scattered throughout upcoming pages). Might you say the same about your life, your workplace, your family? If we are courageous enough to own them, we all have our share of issues, those places where we are still learning to deal in more productive ways.

I (JEP) have watched emotions be the total game changer in my own challenges, as I lead people in daily endeavors, and as I observe friends' adventures in leadership. Regularly, hard-working movers and shakers, brilliant university administrators, deep-caring pastors, and oh-so-sharp executives suddenly quit, implode, or personally blow up. Why? This is seldom due to actual deficiencies in acumen for the tasks of the role, lack of right philosophy, or irreconcilable arguments over theological perspective. Most often, there are deep emotional issues at root.

At the risk of sounding jaded—yes, we might label that an emotion—or even somewhat judgmental toward our own tribe, Christians do not typically handle emotions well. Marc Alan Schelske transparently observes his own personal crises and commotion several years ago. "From where I stood, I could see destruction hurtling down the tracks toward me . . . A crash was coming and all because of the way I was living. I'm only in the beginning stages of untangling all of this . . . But one area in particular that was causing pain to me and the people I cared most about was how I managed (or didn't manage) my emotions." Marc proceeds to identify five ideas that he experienced in church growing up, ideas we have typically learned about emotions in church. According to Schelske, these are emphatically *not true at all*. Such false ideas, too often fostered at church, include:

- God doesn't feel emotions.

- Emotions can only lead you into sin.
- Emotions are not spiritual.
- An emotional Christian is a shallow Christian.
- Ignore your emotions and they will go away.

Perhaps you can resonate, having heard or sensed one or more of these concepts being expressed in Christian communities over the years. We will address and aim to debunk many of these ideas across the chapters to come. Marc marvelously concludes, "The church should be at the forefront of helping people in this process . . . God made us as whole beings. Emotions are a part of that."[7]

As people who supposedly thrive on transformation, why do we not wrestle with this inner dimension with greater gravitas and even joyful anticipation of what might emerge? Perhaps deep down, we are scared of what we might discover. Perhaps the prospect of such hard work, both in our own lives and others' experiences, exacerbates our emotional aversion, only throwing us into further commotions and contortions.

Four foundational concepts support all we share in the coming pages and hopefully serve to motivate greater engagement with the emotional realm. For starters, humans are made in the image of God (Gen 1:26-28). Throughout the Scriptures, we encounter God exhibiting genuine emotions, including but not limited to tender compassion, serious anger, deep regret, and jubilant joy. Such expressions are surely more than simply sophisticated anthropomorphisms (a commonly-taught literary device attributing certain biblical language as speaking of God in humanized terms). God as a true person indeed displays genuine attitudes and renders personal evaluation in light of real-time stimuli and events. If emotions appear as real components of God's image, why would we downplay or ignore this facet of his likeness in us?

Second, the classic Hebrew *Shema* (Deut 6:4-5) presents us as *whole* people—heart, soul, and strength—capable and challenged

---

7. Schelske, "5 Things You Learned About Emotion in Church That Aren't True."

toward loving God with *all* we are. When asked to identify the most important commandment, Jesus reiterated the *Shema* (Matt 22:34-40). Such focus from Christ should awaken us to healthier emotional realizations, both for our own emotional good and for those around us.

Let's face it.

Both the image of God and the primacy of the *Shema* grab our attention and draw us deeper into emotional exploration. And both lead to a third foundational, rather simple, yet also profound concept. You routinely stare at your own face in the morning's mirror—men to scrape whiskers, women to brush some color—or you catch your own visage in your vehicle's rearview. You encounter others' faces multiple times each day as you engage in work projects and eat meals together. Researchers have invested great energy in cataloging the facial-emotional phenomenon in both animals and humans.[8] Admittedly, many nonverbal interactions zoom past us as we maneuver on autopilot, yet even our unofficial observations in others' expressions create profound emotional conclusions and connections.

Consider a recent time, in the days following a face-to-face with someone over coffee or a joint work project, when you found yourself confused about someone's reactions, their follow-up or lack thereof. You were probably asking, "What did I miss? Was it something I said? Did I misread her?" Let's face it. We might all increase our relational capacity and overall effectiveness by learning to better read others' emotions with greater sensitivity

> Hard-working movers and shakers, brilliant university administrators, deep-caring pastors, and oh-so-sharp executives suddenly quit, implode, or personally blow up. Why? Most often, there are deep emotional issues at root.

---

8. Charles Darwin's *The Expression of the Emotions in Man and Animals* serves as one of the earliest examples. Paul Ekman and colleagues revived and expanded on Darwin's emotional work later in the twentieth century.

and accuracy. We might also powerfully improve our own emotional health and life skills by recognizing how our own emotions truly impact our coworkers, family members, and friends in the community.

And this leads to our final foundational component propelling our exploration. Better navigation of our emotions will increase our ability to lovingly impact, serve, and bless others. With his creative answer to the Pharisee in Matthew 22, Jesus powerfully linked the *Shema* with the ancient command to "love your neighbor as you love yourself" (Lev 19:18). Those final four words are essential to effectively accomplishing the first three. "As you love yourself." Christ-honoring others-orientation necessitates a growing self-awareness and developing emotional savvy. Peter Scazzero astutely observes:

> Emotionally unhealthy leaders tend to be unaware of what is going on inside them. And even when they recognize a strong emotion such as anger, they fail to process or express it honestly and appropriately. They ignore emotion-related messages their body may send—fatigue, stress-induced illness, weight gain, ulcers, headaches, or depression. They avoid reflecting on their fears, sadness, or anger. They fail to consider how God might be trying to communicate with them through these "difficult" emotions.[9]

Though humans were originally shaped in our Creator's image, the fall of humans and the resulting curse significantly skewed our ability to not only personally emote in the healthiest ways but also to skillfully read others' emotions. As a result, we find ourselves in need of a remedy—a work of renovation, a way to re-learn. Honestly, we need nothing short of emotional redemption, both for our own good and for others.

M. Robert Mulholland describes spiritual formation as "a process of being conformed to the image of Christ for the sake of others."[10] We find it empowering to recognize the four distinct

---

9. Scazzero, *The Emotionally Healthy Leader*, 27.
10. Mulholland, *Invitation to a Journey*, 15.

features in Mulholland's description: (1) a process (2) of being conformed (3) to the image of Christ (4) for the sake of others. Thankfully, Mulholland's delineation of such steps in spiritual formation affirms that we can personally experience *a process* of transformation, restoring again the image of God through Jesus' work in us. And notice carefully, there's marvelously more. Pursuing this emotional process is not just good for *you*. It's so very good for the *others* God places in front of your face each day.

In the coming chapters, we will go exploring through a set of heartfelt, soul-stirring conversations. Both of us are writing from the backdrop of various experiences in counseling, formal and informal, with people in numerous fields. As a result, we have heard these sincere heart cries in multiple conversations across many years. Intriguingly, the same deep sentiments emerge from ancient stories, now millennia-old. We will journey with a Hebrew family from ancient Israel, facing their own all-out rough and tumble of life commotions. Sprinkled throughout our retelling of their journey, we will also converse with one of the most complex, emotionally challenged leaders from the early days of the Christian movement. And our trek will be complemented by the examples of several other unique personages, both historical and contemporary. This adventure will include a robust mix of sociological, theological, historical, and psychological trails. As we travel, we will likely discover more about our own emotional makeup as well as our precious opportunities to impact coworkers, family, clients, and friends with Christ-focused, transformational work.

Collin Richardson, number ten, grabbed his bat and turned to his teammates who were still stewing and fuming in the dismal dugout. "Come on, Pirates! Let's do this! We've come back before. We'll do it again. It's rally time!" In the moments that followed, two batters walked, finding their way onto base. When Collin stepped up to the plate, he sported the goofiest grin, put on some serious swag, and resoundingly crushed the ball into outer orbit. Two runs scored, and thus began our biggest comeback of the season. It is not overstating the case one iota. This ten-year-old slugger's giant swing and pervasively contagious smile proved to be the game changer, transforming his team members' attitudes and the entire outcome of the Pirate's season.

If it works on the baseball field, might such an emotional shift actually work in all the other fields of life? Let's take a walk and eavesdrop on a conversation.

Questions for Reflection and Discussion

1. On a scale of 1 to 10 (with 10 being the highest), how strong do you rank your daily awareness and personal consideration of your own emotional reactions to situations? And *why* do you give yourself such a ranking?

2. In your family as you were growing up, were emotions typically discussed openly with transparency, or were they stuffed and ignored? Recall a story or example that illustrates your answer.

3. Can you recall sensing or hearing any of Schelske's "five false ideas" in your own past experiences in church?

4. What significance do you believe Jesus' reiteration of the *Shema* (Matt 22:34-40) and his correlation to Leviticus 19:18 might have on our understanding and pursuit of emotional health and development?

5. Reflect on Mulholland's definition of spiritual formation. How might these ideas impact emotional development?

CHAPTER TWO

Dark 'n Stormy

No bird soars in a calm.
—WILBUR WRIGHT

The shire, though previously oh-so-tranquil, was now a cacophony of chaos.

The mighty, majestic *Titanic* was sinking.

Winter had overtaken *Narnia*.

Paradise was lost.

These were dismal days, indeed. It was one of the bleakest seasons in the nation's marvelous, messy history. Three women walked a dusty path, heavy with fatigue and gut-wrenching heartache. Their conversation was ripe with regrets, misty memories, and tense anticipation for future steps. *What could have been? What should have been? Now what could our future hold?* Coming to a halt, the oldest of the three—revealing the early hint of wrinkles across her forehead—begged the other two women. "Turn around, go back home! We've been through so much together for these years, but where I'm headed is no place for the two of you." Her own future felt hopeless and fraught with perpetual doubts. Only one thing seemed certain. There would be deeper, darker wrinkles to come. Why should these two join her on this journey, only to be destined for more gloomy days, doomed to such a fear-filled fate?

As with any tale, grasping our travelers' backstory is crucial to understanding the weary dialogue in this opening scene. We might learn *why* such tumultuous circumstances have emerged. If we dare to explore, the very first clause will enlighten us. The story's opening line in Ruth 1 reads:

In the days when the judges judged . . .

What characterized such days? It was not a *sudden* blackening of the sky, as when it seems a storm capriciously arrives out of nowhere. This story unfolds amid a period between the death of Joshua and the rise of Israel's monarchy, the second half of the second millennium B.C.E.[1] Here was the darkest season to date for Israel. While God's people had experienced all of the wondrous potential and shining hope of entering the promised real estate under Moses and Joshua's leadership, conquest and settlement had now become haphazard and miserably fraught with failure. The Israelites' devotion to their God had plunged in a downward spiral,[2] characterized most often by worshipping the gods of those people groups already inhabiting Palestine.

In occasional bright moments, flickers of hope broke through, times when it was evident that "the LORD was with the men of Judah . . ." (Judg 1:19a). Yet even with the appearance of such silver linings, the people's half-hearted responses led to sad reports like "they were unable to drive the people from the plains, because they had chariots fitted with iron" (Judg 1:19b). Whereas their earlier days brimmed abundant with potential, this season was haunted by their inability to thrive.

Plagued by constant enemy oppression, raiders plundered their crops and other resources. At the core, the nation had experienced a systemic crisis in leadership. History recounts,

---
Your struggling business is tanking. It was already your third attempt to make something fly. Now, both your accountant and lawyer have told you that bankruptcy is your only real option. Here are dark days, indeed.
---

1. Dillard and Longman, *An Introduction to the Old Testament*, 120.
2. Ibid., 125.

"They were in great distress. Then the LORD raised up judges, who saved them out of the hands of these raiders. Yet they would not listen to their judges but prostituted themselves to other gods and worshiped them" (Judg 2:15b–17a). Even with God's provision of new leaders to deliver them, a sad, cyclonic cycle commenced. The whirling winds blew again and again with dark oppression from enemy people groups. Light would break through with the arrival of a new judge—a God-appointed hero-savior— followed by the Israelites' plunge into dark disobedience and oppression once again. It was a tedious, dismal cycle of rebellion, oppression, deliverance, rebellion, oppression, *ad nauseam*. Imagine unending episodes of a reality TV series such as *Survivor*—the characters change, but it's the same tedious plot pattern—rolling every night and getting worse across several hundred years. The final verse of the Judges narrative sadly summarizes: "In those days Israel had no king; everyone did as they saw fit" (Judg 21:25).

In one of those down-spinning seasons, such unbridled, *do whatever* approach led to a famine in the land. Parched ground. Dying herds of animals. No harvest. This was a disastrous consequence of God's people's disobedience, matching what the LORD had forecast in the covenant established at Mount Ebal (Deut 27–30). Such lack of provision and failure to thrive was felt across the land.

With the opening lines of our story, we are drawn into the punctuated hunger of this one little clan, comprised of a man named Elimelek, his wife Naomi (the oldest of the three women), and their sons, Mahlon and Kilion. Suddenly, a regional crisis, the starving consequences of collective disobedience, became poignantly personal for this family.

You know what it's like to walk through dark, scary days. There's a stunning discovery—your dreams of having a child are shattered as the doctor enters the room. Before he even speaks, you can read the chart through his downcast eyes and pursed lips.

Or you finally have to admit that your struggling business is actually tanking. You've been struggling with how to tell your spouse and kids. It was already your third attempt to make something fly.

Now, both your accountant and lawyer have told you that bankruptcy is your only real option. Here are dark days, indeed.

Far too many spouses know the nightmare, a shocking revelation—early morning on a computer screen—that the person who pledged to be faithful has been diabolically unfaithful through a porn addiction or live, person-to-person infidelity. Suddenly, you feel a pitch-black, perfect storm of emotions welling up inside you.

Moments versus seasons

Genuine breakthroughs come when we start distinguishing our dark *moments* from dark *seasons*. Consider one example. While golfing with friends Saturday morning, your tee-shot toward the tenth hole was despicable, barely bobbling past the ladies' tee. Your blood pressure boiled and in exasperation, you pitched your driver down the fairway (your driver actually flew further than your golf ball). With both your shots, you looked like a lunatic to the others in your foursome. You realized it, dipping your mood into an even more deplorable condition and deeper self-loathing.

In this situation, let's clarify. You're having *an emotional moment*; it's not a season. But consider a second example. You are the leader of a development network, giving oversight to savings group facilitators in a remote region southwest of Port Au Prince, Haiti. Under routine conditions, the dear people in your communities find it challenging to make ends meet. But this is now the seventh month with scant rainfall. Sugar cane and other crops are struggling to grow. Accompanying this steep agri-slump, current Haitian authorities have managed once again to maneuver in self-serving ways, exacerbating financial pressures. Your region's savings groups and group leaders are feeling the precipitous downturn as group members' contribution levels plunge. In all-out frustration, people begin pointing fingers, and much of the blame seems aimed at you as the overall leader. You're walking through the dark, and it's internally agonizing.

This is a season. Such skill to clarify is a very helpful exercise on the path toward healthier self-control. A dusty, ancient Hebrew proverb says, "A person without self-control is like a city with broken-down walls."[3] If you stop and recognize that your quick flare-up of feelings is momentary—these emotions are actually short-lived, not a long-term cycle of commotions—you are able to label them as such. Take a deep breath, regain your composure, be a big boy or girl, and apologize for throwing your golf club. You can then reframe your perspective for a better golf game on your final eight holes. Say deep inside, "This too shall pass." Such internal processing, repeated very intentionally in similar scenarios over weeks and months to come, will lead you toward stronger emotional responses, better discipline, and healthier self-control.

And when you discover you are facing an all-out dark and stressful season, like the Haitian leader's crisis, the same old proverb can move you toward greater personal analysis and emotional training. Patiently remember Mulholland's insight on spiritual formation we noted in chapter 1. This is assuredly a *process* of being conformed to the image of Christ for the sake of others. Vital to recall, this is a process.

During such fear-filled seasons, we are actually in good company, and we can glean insights from Naomi and her clan. Her husband, Elimelek, led them in a serious flight from the famine, most likely precipitated by all-out desperation and fear. *We're going to starve. We have to run if we're going to survive!* So they ran to Moab, a nearby country, not a part of Israelite territory.

Moab had at least two things going against it. As a people group, their origins were despised, the result of a drunken, incestuous fling between Abraham's nephew, Lot and his older daughter (Gen 19:37). Yes, we can appropriately contort our faces in disgust. In addition to their grotesque beginning, the Moabites had failed to supply resources for the Israelites as they exited Egypt, and the Moabites had paid Balaam to curse the Israelites. As a result, official covenant stipulations forbid them from entering the LORD's assembly, and the Israelites were instructed: "Do not seek a treaty of friendship with them as long as you live" (Deut 23:3-6). With such a sketchy backdrop for Moab, Elimelek and his family's flight

---

3. Proverbs 25:28 in the *New Living Translation*.

to such a repulsive place was likely viewed by many of their fellow Israelites as spiritually questionable, bordering on moral compromise, even treasonous to their faith. Why could they not stay with their own holy people in Bethlehem, their own holy land, and trust God to supply?

Everybody runs.

Under too much stress, under the gun, under pressure for too long, we run. Here is the oh-so-familiar fight-or-flight response. Recent research in neuroscience and emotional studies, especially the work of Joseph LeDoux,[4] has pinpointed the human brain's amygdala as the central processor for frightening experiences. Johnston and Olson synthesize: "Derived from the Greek word for almond, the amygdala is a complex structure made up of 13 or so separate nuclei engaged in a variety of functions . . . The amygdala, which mediates all aspects of fear learning, truly seems to represent the fear module that LeDoux set out to discover."[5] Daniel Goleman, also drawing largely from LeDoux's discoveries, supplies descriptive overview:

> Incoming signals from the senses let the amygdala scan every experience for trouble. This puts the amygdala in a powerful post in mental life, something like a psychological sentinel, challenging every situation, every perception, with but one kind of question in mind, the most primitive: "Is this something I hate? That hurts me? Something I fear?" If so—if the moment at hand somehow draws a "Yes"—the amygdala reacts instantaneously, like a neural tripwire . . . it sends urgent messages to every major part of the brain: it triggers the secretion of the body's fight-or-flight hormones, mobilizes the centers for movement, and activates the cardiovascular system, the muscles, and the gut.[6]

4. LeDoux, *The Emotional Brain* and "The Amygdala" in *Current Biology*, 17.

5. Johnston and Olson, *The Feeling Brain*, 70.

6. Goleman, *Emotional Intelligence*, 16.

Dark 'n Stormy

On an early-morning walk with my (JEP) Golden Retriever, Brody, we suddenly encountered an oh-so-curious, youthful critter sporting a jet-black body and a thick white racing stripe. Scurrying from the brush on the other side of the road, he was eager to greet us. Brody had never encountered a skunk, so he was mutually interested. Brody's walker, however, had heard friends' stories of working for months to eradicate Pepe Le Pew's pernicious perfume after such a tangle. We did not stay around for the meet and greet. My neural "almond" and related synapses tripped all my wires. I started shouting and yanking on the dog leash with all my might, tearing back up the road. I know firsthand, the amygdala works, and our rendezvous was proof. Everybody runs.

Goleman delineates more of the amygdala's work, as it sends signals that tell the brainstem to fix the face in a fearful expression, increase blood pressure and heart rate, prepare muscles to react as needed, and even sort relevant cortical memories that might prove helpful in the crisis. Supplying further synthesis, Goleman explains,

> LeDoux's work revealed how the architecture of the brain gives the amygdala a privileged position as an emotional sentinel, able to hijack the brain . . . sensory signals from eye or ear travel first in the brain to the thalamus, and then—across a single synapse—to the amygdala; a second signal from the thalamus is routed to the neocortex—the thinking brain. This branching allows the amygdala to begin to respond *before* the neocortex . . . LeDoux's research is revolutionary for understanding emotional life because it is the first to work out neural pathways for feelings that bypass the neocortex. Those feelings that take the direct route through the amygdala include our most primitive and potent; this circuit does much to explain the power of emotion to overwhelm rationality.[7]

The amygdala takes center stage in Goleman's popular concept of emotional intelligence, with vital implications not only for

---

7. Ibid., 17.

finding courage in crisis situations, but also for our training toward healthier emotional responses in a catalog of life arenas. Such responses include navigating personal motivation, delaying impulsive behaviors and short-term gratification, taming anger and aggression, regulating personal moods—even preventing depression—as well as learning to empathize with others and cultivating stronger hope. Most notably, Goleman is an avid optimist regarding the potential to create emotional literacy in children through an expanded mission for teachers at school and parents at home.[8]

> This puts the amygdala in a powerful post in mental life, something like a psychological sentinel, challenging every situation, every perception, with but one kind of question in mind, the most primitive: "Is this something I hate? That hurts me? Something I fear?"
>
> —Daniel Goleman

A teen was out of breath from running. Doggedly pursued by younger boys, one of those rascally characters was the young man's own brother. Now they had him cornered on a long bridge that spanned a deep gully filled with pine trees of assorted sizes and shapes. He certainly dreaded being caught by those younger boys and once again being taunted as a failure. He looked over the side of the bridge and assessed one of the trees as his last desperate hope. He jumped! Three days later, in a hospital, he awoke from his coma. His foolhardy brush with death would mean a long painful recovery. Nevertheless, his pursuers had not officially caught him, a realization that yielded him some scant sense of triumph.

This same young man continued to experience a full dose of failure and deep, dark depression for most of his life. We might wonder how this could be true. After all, he was born in a palatial mansion, the grandson of a famous duke. As a small child, he possessed a wonderful collection of toys that included a real steam engine and over a thousand toy soldiers. He had a personal nurse and later his own governess. The lad worshiped his beautiful mother and idolized his father. His famous aristocratic family was one of the most highly regarded in history.

8. Ibid., 273–281.

However, he was a sickly, frail boy. Many people noticed that his body seemed ill-proportioned. His head appeared too large for the rest of his strangely-shaped body. He spoke with a slight lisp. Although he adored his parents, they neglected him for their own selfish, aristocratic interests. His mother told her friends that she loved horses but despised children. By age seven, he was tagged as a "difficult child" and sent away to boarding school. At school, he did poorly in his studies. He was at the bottom of his class and was often bullied by others. When he entered his teens, it was evident that he was not college material, so his parents sent him to a military academy. At the academy, he did well and began to enjoy himself. He entered a happy and successful season.[9]

Unfortunately, his entire life was filled with recurring periods of failure in a vast array of areas. Compounding all of his troubles, or perhaps because of them, he suffered from what he later called "my black dog." This black dog was his way of describing his dark, lengthy bouts of deep depression. The dog hounded him for all ninety years of his illustrious life.[10]

This is the man whom many have called the greatest figure of the twentieth century. He inspired his country to endure terrible hardship and the frightening, horrific years of the Nazi terror. His speeches rallied a world in the darkest days of World War II. His determination to settle for nothing short of victory at all cost is believed by some to be one of the major reasons Hitler and the Nazis were eventually defeated.

Churchill always believed he had a specific destiny. He believed he was born for some great reason or cause. Who can say for certain? But eminent historians and psychologists believe that perhaps it was his own experiences with rejection, fear, failure, and such dark days of despondency that taught Sir Winston Churchill the skills needed to overcome, to snatch victory from the jaws of defeat.

Employing big picture reflection, we can join with experts across multiple disciplines—including theology, psychology,

9. Churchill, *My Early Life*, vii–xix and 1–60.
10. Storr, *Churchill's Black Dog, Kafka's Mice and Other Phenomena of the Human Mind*, vii–x and 1–50.

biology, and sociology—affirming that such intentional emotional development to overcome is still possible for "kids" of all ages. Let's identify some starter steps for our own journey in this personal process of change and growth.

Deeply own your own emotions.

Journeying toward better emotional health requires patience to embrace the process and the courage to step into decisive ownership. Aiming to help us grasp such a step-at-a-time process, Peter Scazerro shares a simplified explanation of Benjamin Bloom's famous taxonomy relating how people learn and change. Steps in the process involve the following levels of "getting" a concept or value:

- Awareness. You become aware there is a problem or issue to address.
- Ponder. You actively seek to understand via reading, listening, and other research.
- Value. You begin to believe this is important and you dabble with new behaviors.
- Prioritize. You start to shift your entire life to integrate this new value/concept.
- Own. You begin to base your decisions and actions on the value/concept.[11]

At level five, you begin taking life-changing steps in your emotional development. Deeply owning your overall feelings and responses means you start making decisions and choosing actions that actually reflect your more passionate pursuit of emotional health. Specifically related to your fears, you own up to your own propensity to run.

If you've been scampering like the cartoon characters Scooby Doo and Shaggy instead of staying and facing your fears in bold faith, admit it. "The role and overall responsibilities in my job have

---

11. Scazerro, *The Emotionally Healthy Leader*, 43–44.

grown overwhelming. That's why I've been hunting for something else, spending bigger blocks of my afternoons on social media, avoiding colleagues whenever possible, and otherwise slacking." You can courageously own these behaviors, boldly call them what they are, and commit to change. Or perhaps you need to admit: "My marriage seemed too difficult so I ran off with the other person. I've actually felt more and more miserable ever since the initial thrill of the fling wore off." Some of us, when the going gets tough due to meager pay or over-ample conflict, actually pull an Elimelek. We suddenly pull up stakes and move our entire family to another land. Fear gets the best of us, and we flee the scene.

There is something very healthy about openly admitting this inside your own soul, both with God and with others. "I tend to run," or "I've been running." Only then are you ready to step into more courageous attitudes and actions. Owning your emotions is a vitally important step in the process of personal training toward healthier responses.

Take selfish choices and consequences seriously.

Here's another key insight for processing fear-filled seasons. We do not live under the old covenant of the ancient Israelites. Instead in our day, because of Christ, we are oh-so-privileged to experience God's amazingly lavish grace. We should not expect or dread the same curses to boomerang just like the Israelites living under those old stipulations in Deuteronomy. However, we should live with the sober anticipation that God's overarching principles still hold true. "A man reaps what he sows" (Gal 6:7). Disobedient, selfish, sinful choices bring consequences. Play with fire, and you get burned. Step out in traffic, and you get hit. Overspend, and you go in debt. Abuse your body, and you suffer. And here's the kicker. *Your self-centered choices never just impact you.* The collective idolatry of Israel resulted in dismal days for individuals and whole families, like Naomi and her tribe. Self-indulgent living always ripples out to affect your clan, your coworkers, and your congregation.

EmotiConversations

But not *too* seriously

Let's be clear, very clear, on this point of differentiation. Not every dark day is the result of your own choices—*your* sins, mishaps, weaknesses, or even your own goofy idiosyncrasies. In fact, quite often, we experience frightening, gloomy circumstances, and other people or past events are at fault. We're caught up in other people's messy, stormy situations. We end up catching the dismal results of their self-centeredness, rebellion, or half-hearted choices. When you are faced with dark and dismal fears, the origins of which are not your own foibles, character flaws, or reckless making, discipline yourself to differentiate, to emotionally *reframe*.

Slow down enough to analyze and reframe. For many years, a water-stained, dusty lithograph of the pilgrims' landing at Plymouth Rock hung at a sloppy angle from a thin wire on a nail in my grandfather's garage (JEP's Grandpa Hall, HHP's father). Several years after Grandpa's death, we recognized some potential in the old print. It was wrapped in a dingy, dark frame. Carefully removing the black and white litho, we discovered the water stain was not nearly as bad as originally thought. Lightly blowing away dust, we found that what had appeared to be smudged now emerged as crisp, bold lines of that historic scene at Plymouth. Best of all, we sanded and then refinished the frame. Beautiful, golden oak lines emerged. We even carefully brushed brass-colored paint into the fancy inset beads adorning the frame's inner edge. Once the print was replaced in the newly restored frame, it proved seriously stunning to behold. This vintage piece of art now hangs in my (JEP's) family room and proves to be a constant conversation piece.[12]

Reframing is a serious game changer. Say it to yourself and say it often: "This dark mess was not my making." Let go of every inch of self-blame and guilt. Yes, it feels dismal and ugly, but it is not your fault—especially when other people have been haphazardly doing whatever seems right in their own sight. Seriously, this dark mess was not your making. Herein lies a crucial step, an

---

12. See the reframed Plymouth picture at http://johneltonpletcher.com/plymouth-pic-reframing/

emotional exercise leading toward healthier responses. With Christ's help, you can retrain and reframe your thought patterns. Repeat it as a holy mantra: "This dark mess was not my making."

Sometimes, we face such a treacherous wake from others' dismal choices. In tandem, there are numerous times when our dark seasons' cause can be identified as none other than the ugly spillover of the original curse of sin back in the Garden of Eden (Gen 3). So much suffering—from natural disasters to debilitating childhood diseases and numerous calamities that leave us asking desperate, unending "why on God's green earth" questions—holds a general origin in the overarching, ghastly curse of sin in Genesis' third chapter.[13] While this explanation for suffering's origin does not magically transform how we feel when facing tragic events, it can help us reframe, to remember that this dark scene is not our fault. Even equipped with the ability to blame *sin and the fall*, we still ask big questions regarding God's purposes. It is vital for us to resist trite, quick, cliché answers, to instead embrace the multi-dimensionality of God's transformational aims in our lives.[14] Sometimes, our dark seasons hold profoundly higher, deeper, and more far-reaching purposes that seem mysteriously out of reach.

> When you are faced with dark and dismal fears, the origins of which are not your own foibles, character flaws, or reckless making, discipline yourself to differentiate, to emotionally *reframe*. Reframing is a serious game changer.

The ghost in the darkness

Wind was howling. Waves were still crashing. It had been a treacherous night at sea, and though it was almost dawn, blackness still cloaked the water. Jesus' young apprentices had been doing their

---

13. For further insights, see Ralph O. Muncaster's booklet *Why Does God Allow Suffering?*

14. For an astute, creative, multifaceted approach to processing suffering, see Robert C. Palmer and Heather Palmer Welesko's *The Diamond of Adversity: A Theology of Suffering.*

best to ride out the storm. As if circumstances were not bad enough, suddenly, they saw what appeared to be a phantom walking near them atop the water. "When the disciples saw him walking on the lake, they were terrified. 'It's a ghost,' they said, and cried out in fear" (Matt 14:26). Christ himself spoke to them. "Take courage! It is I. Don't be afraid." Movingly, Jesus placed himself at the center of their storm and the very center of his reassuring, challenging words to them.

As one of Christ's leaders-in-training, ever-impulsive Peter chose to push the envelope. "Lord if it's you, tell me to come to you on the water." Christ did not appear fazed by Pete's audacity. "Come." And Peter went on the craziest walk of his life while the storm was still raging. For at least a few minutes—we are not told exactly how long—Peter stayed up. "But when he saw the wind, he was afraid and, beginning to sink, cried out, 'Lord, save me!'" (Matt 14:30) Christ reached out his hand, rescued Peter, and challenged him toward greater faith. Once Christ climbed into the boat, the wind subsided and all of the disciples worshipped him, recognizing Jesus in a more profound way as the Son of God.

Reframe, refocus, and return.

What a stunning scene packed with God's mysterious, formative purposes for his team. Peter was experiencing an intensely personal season of transformational training. Christ was leading him through a process, and one of the primary exercises Peter was learning was how to reframe—to deliberately refocus his vision—to choose bigger faith in the face of dark and scary seasons. Such courageous choices would become essential to his ministry for the sake of others during the early, formative days of Christ's church. It is highly instructive that Jesus offers the disciples *himself*. "Take courage. *It is I*. Don't be afraid." Ironically, the supposed ghost was now their source of confidence, courage, and ability to walk above the waves.

Facing great fear in our darkest seasons does not mean we are failures. Every person on the planet experiences fear. But continuing to run from God's faith-strengthening process—refusing to retrain our neural-spiritual eyes—increases our potential of failing and missing out on the greater growth God has for us. Staying laser-focused on Jesus—taking courage from him—that's our emotional game changer.

Today, Christ oh-so-graciously offers each of us a return. What steps will we take next on our journey of emotional transformation? Having experienced these dark "days when the judges judged," it was time for a new walk. Naomi was returning, heading back to her people in the land of Judah. The darkness and loss for their tribe was even more personalized and profound. There is so much more to their story. Still weighed down with heavy hearts, reeling with the sting of biting loss, what next steps would Naomi and her daughters-in-law take? Scazzero encourages us as we continue the journey:

> Mature spiritual leadership is forged in the crucible of difficult conversations, the pressure of conflicted relationships, the pain of setbacks, and dark nights of the soul. Out of these experiences, we come to understand the complex nature of our inner world. Moreover, as we develop new practices and rhythms robust enough to withstand the pressures that leadership exerts on the inner life, we naturally become stronger and more effective leaders. And we move on from simply affirming truth and wisdom to owning and applying what we know.[15]

In the pages to come, let's join their difficult conversations, lean closer, listen deeper, and discover how to grow stronger through grief and loss.

---

15. Scazzero, *The Emotionally Healthy Leader*, 50.

EMOTICONVERSATIONS
Questions for Reflection and Discussion

1. What most astounds you about such dark "days when the judges judged?" Can you see any transferable lessons for today?

2. Identify a time recently when you have experienced an emotional *moment*. Do you find this concept of differentiating between an emotional *moment* and an emotional *season* to be helpful? Why or why not?

3. How might you apply the dusty Hebrew proverb (25:28) to a current scenario? How might such wisdom better inform your own current emotional responses?

4. Do you find this perspective-shaping skill of *reframing* to be potentially helpful? Why or why not? In what situations might you currently employ this concept?

5. What impresses you about Peter's scary walk on the water? How do Jesus' words to the disciples challenge and encourage you in this season?

CHAPTER THREE

Oh, Good Grief!

When you come out of the storm, you won't be the same person who walked in. That's what the storm's all about.

—HARUKI MURAKAMI

Ding! The breakfast table vibrates for a split second, and my (JEP) teenager grabs his phone. As he voraciously consumes his friend's text, he skillfully scoops another spoonful of Raisin Bran and chuckles at what she has texted. Ironically, his actual face instantaneously reflects many of the symbolic, cartoon-like faces appearing on his screen. He and his friends habitually express their various feelings and moods not just through words, but also via facial characters in the form of icons. With another mouthful of cereal and another ding of his phone, my son is sporting an enormous grin once again. (Yes, Dad detects at least a wink of flirtation being exchanged.)

It's fascinating to consider. Our methods of daily, real-time communication via technology have morphed into a multi-faceted blend of self-portrayal on screens. Such interaction involves not only the writer's thoughts through keyed words, but also the writer's overall tone via emoticons. These caricatures serve to communicate a catalog of feelings a person might express in various scenarios. Just take a look at your own phone's texting features for a moment and consider the vast array of choice expressions in the palm of your hand.

While such communication methods would appear to represent a relatively recent trend, our current-day craze over emoticons actually holds primal roots in the earliest days of emotional research. Experts worked to identify specific expressions, especially those commonly expressed throughout virtually every cultural background around the globe. Paul Ekman conducted collaborative experiments along with Wallace Friesen and Richard Sorenson. Their study presented research participants with pictures of faces that conveyed emotional expressions, and they were asked to assign to each face one of six labels: *anger, happiness, fear, surprise, disgust,* or *sadness*. Conducting this experiment on multiple continents led to the early conclusion that these six "basic" emotional expressions are readily recognizable everywhere, thus establishing a universality of basic emotions.[1]

Similar research by various emotions theorists has generated great controversy as well as different lists of basic emotions. Johnston and Olson supply a table delineating the theorists and their unique emotion lists. Such variety in various names often employed for the primary emotions include: fear, terror, anger, rage, distress, anguish, sadness, enjoyment, joy, surprise, disgust, shame, humiliation, anticipation, care, play, panic, and grief.[2]

From bad to worse—to worst

When we rejoin Naomi and her daughters-in-law on the return to Judah, their continued interaction reveals an equally exhaustive list of emotional reactions. Many of the above-listed, primary emotions probably showed up on their faces, including deep grief over horrific loss. Before we actually listen to more of their chatter on the road, there are just a few more important pieces of backstory to consider.

Extremely intriguing and vital to this ancient story is the role of names, both the people and their places. We will revisit this

---

1. Ekman, Friesen, and Sorenson, "Pan-cultural elements," *Science,* 164, 86–88.

2. Johnston and Olson, *The Feeling Brain,* 51.

important feature across our discussion, but for starters, note the family patriarch. His name, *Elimelek*, actually means "my God is king." Such a distinct name held importance in that ancient setting for the original cast of characters. And this name, shared at the story's outset, serves as a powerful reminder to us that as the ruling monarch, God is in control of the story.[3] God is always king, always in control, totally faithful, and worthy of his people's trusting adoration through all the varying twists and turns on our journey.

> How could anything possibly get worse? But like a kid with a "KICK ME" sign plastered to her back, she got kicked again. We've all discovered it, often multiple times. Life can suddenly accelerate and turn from worse to worst.

All that breaks loose for this Hebrew family might cause us to question the validity of such meaning in Elimelek's name. Is God truly king and in control? During the opening years after the family settled in Moab, life went from bad—the serious famine—to worse. Elimelek died. The original storyteller stated this in a rather matter-of-fact manner. No specific details were supplied regarding his death, but Carolyn James reflects the far-reaching gravity for the family:

> Elimelech's death hurled Naomi into grief that ebbed and flowed for the rest of her life. But for Naomi, as for other widows with children, there was little time to think of herself or to nurse her own grief because of the pressing needs of her two sons. The death of Elimelech catapulted her into the ranks of single parents—a daunting task in any era or culture. At least Naomi still had her sons.[4]

Soon, both sons married Moabite women. At first glance, we might assume this is a beautiful development. In reality, their marriages to Orpah and Ruth were fraught with rugged spiritual and societal complications. Carolyn James supplies further insight: "The problem for Naomi, however, wasn't that the girls her sons brought home were less than perfect. Ruth and Orpah weren't even

   3. Fentress-Williams, *Ruth*, 40.
   4. James, *The Gospel of Ruth*, 40.

in the running. As Moabites—pagan worshipers of Chemosh, a god that demanded child sacrifice—these women represented a believing Israelite mother's worst fears."[5] If moving to Moab had originally raised eyebrows for family and friends back in Israel (as we noted in chapter 2), marrying Moabite women certainly would have sent tongues wagging back in Judah. Such intermarriage was terribly taboo for God's people.

Following the famine, their run to relocate, and the death of Elimelek, how could anything possibly get worse for Naomi? But like a kid with a "KICK ME" sign plastered to her back, she got kicked again. Life took another downward spiral plunge. After approximately ten years living in Moab, "both Mahlon and Kilion also died" (Ruth 1:5a). We've all discovered it, often multiple times. Life can suddenly accelerate and turn from worse to worst.

Close to home and bittersweet

Our own family's recent decade includes similar, bad-to-worse scenarios. Seven years ago, Grandma Hall—loved matriarch, the hold-everybody-together "glue" for our whole tribe— experienced a severe stroke. Sadly, her condition did not improve. She held on for over ten days, but rather suddenly, a small handful of immediate family members were wrapped around her hospice bed. We had received the call late evening around eleven o'clock. Gram had taken a sudden turn and was close to passing. For approximately forty-five minutes, we stood vigil. While speaking words of lavish love, admiration, and appreciation, we passionately prayed over her.

Old movie scenes often show a dying person departing peacefully, and perhaps you have heard stories from family and friends of a loved one who passes with a tranquil repose, maybe even a smile. Unfortunately, this was not such a scene. Though hospice nurses did a beautiful job administering pain meds and keeping her as comfortable as possible, Gram gasped for air and kept working to draw up every breath she could muster. It was

5. Ibid., 41.

seriously tough to watch. Tenacious and determined, her painstaking toil elicited our best attempts to share comforting words. "Go ahead. Go be with Grandpa. Find Aunt Ruth and Cousin Grace. They're waiting. Go ahead, and we'll see you soon."

We spoke such words while gushing buckets of tears and gulping our own short breaths. It was sincerely one of the most bittersweet moments of our lives. With Grandma Hall's final breaths, we had the sincere privilege of actually sensing when she walked into Christ's arms. It was palpable for each of us surrounding her in those moments. She was home.

Later, we all agreed. It was a serious privilege to be with her for those final moments, but the vigil was heart wrenching. We also spoke candidly together in subsequent conversations. We would not necessarily sign up with enthusiasm to experience such a painful and poignant scene again.

Shockingly, there would be another very similar evening. Just three years later, we again conducted a watch-and-wait, cry-and-pray, comfort-and-cheer vigil, this time for Kenny (HHP's husband, JEP's dad). It was the culmination of his courageous, five-year battle with prostate cancer. On that cold February evening, the scene was eerily familiar. Dad also worked hard for each last breath. Finally, with some great encouragement from all of us, he stepped over the threshold and arrived at home with his Savior.

Reality was, we had already felt kicked again and again as we walked through a long season of grief. Now, we found ourselves asking big questions. "Why did either Gram or Dad have to experience such suffering? Why did God want us present for those dreadful final moments—should anyone really have to see that? What might be God's purposes in such deep and painful loss?" When we grieve, we all ask big questions such as these, both with God and with other people.

Naomi's deep loss and grief are captured in this synthesis: ". . . so that the woman was left without her two sons and her husband" (Ruth 1:5b, ESV). At first glance, this seems like a desperately gloomy report. However, intriguing literary artistry is intentionally at work in the storyteller's choice of phraseology. E. John Hamlin explains:

> The Hebrew verb translated 'left' is the root of the noun translated 'remnant.' . . . Naomi was, however, not only the sole *survivor* of her family; she was also a sign of hope. The bold affirmation of the book of Ruth is that Naomi 'the woman' (Ruth 1:5), with neither husband nor sons, is in fact *the remnant who will return*.[6]

Hence, what initially appears to be a devastatingly despondent, grief-stricken scene actually offers us a serious foretaste, a teaser of potential hope.

Yes, for Naomi, there was a glimmering prelude, a glimpse of real hope with such *remnant* language, but we cannot just quickly whisk away the grim nature of the scene. There is still Naomi's dismal backdrop, including wayward, do-whatever-they-want people, the starvation nation, her fear-filled, run-for-Moab family, and the tragic loss of her husband. And don't miss the unstated, yet oh-so-evident familial dilemma—both couples had been grappling with infertility.[7] And as if all this was not bad enough, the family faced a double-whammy with the death of both sons. Such dreadful pile-up of painful circumstances placed the family line in all-out jeopardy. Big questions. Is God truly king and in control? How in the world could God ever bring hope out of such grief and loss? Naomi, whose name meant "sweet one," now felt the soul-biting sting of bitterness.

Many faces of grief

Grief readily kicks us in a variety of incarnations, most typically arriving in tandem with life's serious frowns and otherwise downcast facial expressions—the kind that might last for seasons, embedding the deepest wrinkles. Les Carter and Frank Minrith

---

6. Hamlin, *Surely There Is A Future*, 10–11.

7. For explanation of these literary dynamics of barrenness, see Sakenfeld, *Ruth*, 20.

define grief as "the emotion of loss, typified by feelings of anguish, sorrow, regret, and longing for something that is gone."[8]

When have you recently observed the faces of grief in your own experiences? Grief can emerge over a failed marriage, loss of your long-term employment or other financial security, a specialist's grim diagnosis, death of a close family member or friend, or utter frustration over business dreams that suddenly disintegrate. Such feelings of loss are often accompanied by repeated patterns of reminiscing for the better days, deepest disillusionment, and personal labeling of oneself as "incomplete" or "a big failure." And our grief often includes a pervasive dose of just-can't-shake-it self-pity. We often end up frozen in place, stuck in our tracks. Tim King and Frank Martin observe:

> The story of fear has done more harm . . . It has immobilized more people—both believers and unbelievers—and left more lives fractured and isolated than all other religious deceptions combined. Think about what fear says to God. It tells him, "You're not big enough. The Cross of Christ doesn't cast a wide enough shadow. Your promises can't be trusted."[9]

Naomi wrestled with a full dose of grief's tag-along feelings, including psychological fractures, relational isolation, as well as feeling frozen in such a dreadful season, struggling to move forward.

While still in Moab, Naomi heard that God had visited his people back home in Judah. God's rescue arrived—a new season with bumper crops and signs of a bountiful harvest. Naomi responded to this marvelous news by choosing to get up and get moving—to make a life-altering return. Her stormy story reflects solid seeds of faith-filled hope in her God. Amid such grievous loss, she certainly wrestled with lethargy, deep sorrow, and probably even bouts of depression. Yet even with such clouds of despair still hovering, she chose to exercise starter-steps of faith, to embark

---

8. Carter and Minrith, *The Freedom from Depression Workbook*, 99.
9. King and Martin, *Furious Pursuit*, 32.

on her own transformative journey from death-filled Moab to life-giving Judah.[10]

Her daughters-in-law, Ruth and Orpah, accompanied Naomi on those early steps, and their conversation reveals that Naomi was indeed experiencing the full onslaught—many of the typical grief descriptors, and then some. Had she been able to text, we might imagine an abrupt onslaught of emoticons. Her messages would have carried caricatures with downward frowns, drooped eyebrows, and gushing tears. But at some point on her screen, we would have also seen icons expressing faith, hope, and forward momentum.

> Grief can emerge over a failed marriage, loss of your long-term employment or other financial security, a specialist's grim diagnosis, death of a close family member or friend, or utter frustration over business dreams that suddenly disintegrate.

When facing grief, both your own and others', resist every urge—both self-induced and pushed by others—to rush your responses. Quick fixes and pithy spiritual platitudes are rarely productive. Don't hurry yourself to get over your grief, and be very careful what you say to friends and family when they are experiencing loss. H. Norman Wright cites a number of our well-intended but too-often unhelpful, potentially even pain-producing clichés.

- Big boys don't cry.
- You've just got to get ahold of yourself.
- Cheer up.
- Time will heal.
- Life goes on.
- This is the work of the devil.
- Count your blessings.
- God never gives us more than we can handle.

10. Hamlin, *Surely There Is a Future*, 13–14.

- I know just how you feel.
- You can have more children.
- If there is anything I can do, just call me.[11]

We dare not hurry ourselves and loved ones to quickly process grief, to "just get over it," and get on with life. But we can, like Naomi, choose to get back up, step forward, and trust God with bigger hope. When you are ready, you can choose to walk a fresh path. Like Naomi and her daughters-in-law, you can focus on God's provision for your brighter future. You can boldly embrace your fresh start toward a deeper faith—an overcoming, hope-filled trust to match your deepest grief.

Blocking and shoving

In their original, sidesplitting blockbuster, Shrek and Donkey are camping outside, guarding Princess Fiona as she sleeps in the cave. Staring at the stars and moon, Donkey decides to play therapist and confront Shrek about his threat to build a wall around his swamp to keep everyone out. In their terse, back-and-forth interchange, Donkey makes the now famous and oft-quipped statement (at least it's quoted often in the Pletcher house), "You cut me deep, Shrek. You cut me real deep!" With a sullen face and folded arms, Shrek abruptly rolls to his other side. Donkey gets in his face. "You're blocking." "No, I'm not!" Shrek adamantly denies as he rolls to his other side. "Yes, you are!" Donkey retorts.

While Naomi's initial steps toward Judah reveal some seriously positive faith and seeds of hope, her next text reveals the ongoing reality of mixed emotions. There was a lingering, raw messiness in the face of her grief. "Go back home." Shrek-style, Naomi was blocking. As she shoved them to head back to Moab, she also expressed heartfelt wishes for God to grant them new husbands, employing the ancient Hebrew term *hesed*. This rich term denotes loyal, covenant love, a ferociously devoted kindness. "May

---

11. Wright, *Helping Those Who Hurt*, 32–33.

God give back to you the same level of faithful, loving kindness which you have expressed to your husbands and to me." Naomi's recognition of such faithful love proved foundational, an early echo of God's character expressed throughout the story's characters as the tale unfolds.[12] Naomi then kissed them and cried aloud with them. No doubt about it, the moment was emotion-packed (Ruth 1:8–9). They met Naomi's push with their own declaration of resolve, still insisting they would return to Judah with her.

Naomi foisted her blockade higher by playing out a potential scenario. "I am way too old to have another husband and give birth to more sons. Just suppose, girls, even if there was some hope for me—if I married a new man tonight and gave birth to sons—you could not wait that long for the boys to grow up." Although Naomi's faith-filled steps toward her land of Judah revealed seeds of hope, her big shove toward Orpah and Ruth evidenced how much she was still wrestling. Her's was an all-out mix of emotions. Thick text in verse thirteen demonstrates a serious depth of feeling and also oh-so-authentic self-awareness: "No, my daughters. It is more bitter for me than for you, because the LORD'S hand has turned against me."

Here is a bubbling stew on her soul's back burner, truly a messy mix of feelings that sounds all-too-familiar to many of us who have also walked this grief journey. Katharine Sakenfeld observes,

> In considering Naomi's bitterness, one must come to terms with more than the socio-economic marginalization of a childless widow in Israelite culture. The reality of the loss of a beloved spouse or of a child, or children, let alone all of one's immediate blood family, is devastating emotionally to most people in most cultures . . . Readers of this story who have grieved deeply themselves or who have accompanied a close friend or relative on that path will more easily grasp the way in which this entire

---

12. Hamlin, *Surely There Is A Future*, 16–17.

book may be read as a story about Naomi as much as one about Ruth.[13]

Naomi readily admitted, instead of pleasant, life's thick soup tasted very bitter. "No one else feels what I'm going through." She can't resist saying it: "God is to blame. I've felt his heavy hand." Such bitter tastes are very normal, genuine cries of grief. And take heart—they are typically expressed by the best of us.

Catharsis at work

How often do we self-protect, block others, or otherwise try to hide what we're really feeling, unwilling to let others see us grieve? Especially at the office, in the shop, or out on the production floor—how preposterous would that be, to let others know you are grieving?

Kristin Brown courageously ponders four principles for better grieving in the workplace. She urges—

- Don't feel ashamed to show your grief. You may be worried about crying at odd times, like in the middle of a meeting. Give yourself permission to be a little less poised.

- Avoid making major decisions while grieving. Some decisions may be unavoidable. But for those that seem optional, it's best to wait until your thinking is less clouded.

- Don't interrupt or abbreviate your season of grief, but productive work is healthy. Both hope and joy can co-exist with sorrow and sadness. Putting your hand to the plow with tears coming down your face is not a bad thing.

- Share in the sorrow of those who are grieving around you. People in grief want to know that others are, in a sense, carrying some of the sorrow that they are experiencing.[14]

---

13. Sakenfeld, *Ruth*, 36.
14. Brown, "Why We Can—and Should—Grieve at Work."

Oh, Good Grief!

I (HHP) had been warned not to return to my hectic work pace too soon after my husband's death. However, I couldn't stand the thought of sitting alone in a now too-empty, too-quiet house. For five long years, I watched and grieved as the life and vitality were drained from my husband by cancer. Ken was a hardworking Christian man who faithfully loved and served the Lord with every inch of his fiber. It really defied my reason that a kind and gracious God would allow him such suffering. Now I felt set adrift on a sea of grief. "Buck up. Get busy. Don't dwell on it. Get back to work." I admonished myself and stuffed back waves of emotion.

A tap sounded on my office door. I looked up to see a large, fifty-something man, camouflage hat in hand, standing there. I put on a bright smile and stood up from my desk. Extending my hand for my trained professional handshake, I said, "Hi, I'm Holly. Grab a chair. How can I help you this morning?" The man's face turned to a strange shade of scarlet and grey that blended with his worn Ohio State tee shirt. Beads of perspiration broke out on his forehead, and for a brief second, I wondered if I might need to grab my phone and dial 911 for him. "I'm Rick," he gulped. "I'll tell you straight up, I'm embarrassed to be here. I'm so mad at myself. I feel like a total failure. But I gotta do something. You are my last chance for help."

Tears welled up in the eyes of this big manly man. Fifteen years ago I would have sat down beside Rick and put my arms around his shoulders. Contemporary professionalism, strict policy, and my own wisdom no longer allowed touch in the workplace environment. So, I did what I could and pushed my box of tissues in his direction. "No, God! Not today! I have my own issues. I can't face listening to this man cry on my shoulder." I breathed my silent admonishment to God. I had a pretty good idea what story would follow.

> How often do we block others and try to hide what we're really feeling, unwilling to let others see us grieve? Especially at the office, in the shop, or out on the production floor—how preposterous would that be, to let others know you are grieving?

Since the economy tanked, I had heard these accounts from people like Rick all too often in the last few years. And my hunch was correct again.

Rick dropped out of high school halfway through his senior year. His girlfriend, Carol, was pregnant, and his parents told him he would have to "man up" and marry Carol. He quickly got a job at a local manufacturing plant and was soon making good money. He did not need a high school diploma after all.

As prosperous years rolled along, Rick and Carol had three nice kids, a new vehicle every two years, a boat, and a lovely home. The kids were almost ready to begin college when disaster struck. The plant closed and took their business to Mexico. Rick was out of work. Eventually, his unemployment ran out. Rick faithfully searched for a job, any job. But now, the job market was so tight, and no one would hire him without a high school diploma.

This hard-working, all-American couple had lost their house and vehicles, and now Rick feared he would lose Carol next. His lack of a completed education was Rick's dirty little secret. Carol knew but not the kids. He wanted them to value education and to not follow in his footsteps. Rick had reached rock bottom and was desperate. Sitting there in my office, he simply imploded as the emotions drained out of his big body. Like me, Rick was grieving a loss, and it was taking an emotional toll.

Rick's story does end well. He enrolled in our GED program and completed his classes. After GED graduation, he signed up for an adult vocational training program. Today, he is employed again at an even better job that he seriously loves. Rick has truthfully shared his journey with his children so they will understand his insistence on the importance of education.

Catharsis is the healthy process of releasing and thereby providing relief from strong or repressed emotion. Here is the willingness to authentically roll with what you are feeling, to express it openly, and to experience the healing work that results from such openness. When embraced properly, such cathartic work can actually be used by God *to conform us even more to the image of Christ, for the sake of others.*

After Rick left my office that morning, I closed the office door and had my own meltdown. It would not be the last during the coming months. Nevertheless, each time I emptied yet another tissue box with my tears, I felt a sense of renewal and restoration. Yes, I may have returned to work too soon. But in the process of my daily work, God faithfully brought others into my life. Around me were many folks who were also grieving various kinds of losses and going through emotional tsunamis as a result.

Open now and moving forward

Our water-walking friend, Peter, did his own share of blocking. When Jesus was captivating Peter and calling him to follow, the fumbling fellow gave Christ a serious shove. Out on Galilee, stunned by the enormous catch of fish, Peter blurted out, "Go away from me, Lord; I am a sinful man!" Instead of leaving, Christ lovingly stayed and encouraged him: "Don't be afraid; from now on you will fish for people" (Luke 5:8–10). Christ was filling him with courage and calling him to deeply embrace a way of life *for the sake of others.*

Peter walked courageously forward, followed Jesus, and learned so much about the transformative process, including the role of hope and grief. Decades later, as a tried-and-true, storm-weathered leader, the then-aged Apostle Peter wrote:

> Praise be to the God and Father of our Lord Jesus Christ! In his great mercy he has given us new birth into a living hope through the resurrection of Jesus . . . In all this you greatly rejoice, though now for a little while you may have had to suffer grief in all kinds of trials. These have come so that the proven genuineness of your faith—of greater worth than gold, which perishes even though refined by fire—may result in praise, glory and honor when Jesus Christ is revealed (1 Pet 1:3–7).

Such text reveals, Peter got it! He reached the pivotal point where he could personally say, "Grief is good because of Christ's faith-strengthening outcome in our lives."

How about you? Are you still stuck blaming God? Still blocking others? Or are you open and anticipating, ready to move forward, and genuinely hope-filled regarding God's power to work?

Orpah turned back for Moab and her mother's house. But Ruth, feisty and faithful, dug her sandals deep into the road toward Judah. She proclaimed a ferocious commitment to Naomi and their future journey, further demonstrating God's covenant-style of *hesed*. Shockingly, Ruth even declared a passionate, personal allegiance to Naomi's God (Ruth 1:16–17). Yes, she made an all-out vow, invoking the name of Naomi's LORD, the same God Naomi was questioning and blaming. Don't forget, Ruth was from the other side of the tracks—a forbidden Moabite and a spiritual stranger.

> When embraced properly, such cathartic work can actually be used by God *to conform us even more to the image of Christ, for the sake of others.*

The emotion-battered matriarch surrendered to Ruth's dogged determination. She finally quit blocking. Such openness could not have come at a better time. Their next steps bring them face-to-face with a buzz of new characters, their own serious financial needs, and the all-out challenge to discover deeper answers. Along the faith journey, we are all faced with the challenge. Can we move forward and trust God to truly provide?

Questions for reflection and discussion

1. Can you identify a time when it felt like you had a "KICK ME" sign on your back, when situations seemed to go from bad to worse to worst?

2. Have you experienced a season of deep grief and loss? How would you describe your own mix of emotions?

3. With which pieces of Naomi's journey and feelings can you most readily relate? Why?

4. Do you tend to block others when you're experiencing emotions of grief and loss? Explain your response. What's the big deal about being open and receptive to others?

5. How does *hesed*, God's non-stop loving kindness, prove essential for encouraging hope in the face of grief? When have you seen such strong, faithful, loyal love make a real difference in your life or others' lives?

6. How do Peter's example and words fill you with hope (Luke 5:8–10 and 1 Pet 1:3–7)?

7. Identify several tangible ways you can cultivate greater hope and more genuine faith, both for yourself and for others, when walking through grief and loss.

CHAPTER FOUR

Flourishing in a Financial Crunch

Hope is a projection of the imagination; so is despair. Despair all too readily embraces the ills it foresees; hope is an energy and arouses the mind to explore every possibility to combat them.

—THORNTON WILDER

When you are seriously hungry, developing a hopeful and grateful perspective is extremely challenging. The year was 1931, Great Depression America near Buffalo, New York. On his daily walk to school, a boy trudged through the waist-deep, mid-December snow. He shivered again, pulled his stocking cap tighter, and shoved his hands deeper into the threadbare pockets of his hand-me-down coat. The middle school boy came from a hard-working, upstanding farm family. Like most of the folks in their region, they were now nearly impoverished. Many mornings on this walk to school, the young man felt hungry and very much alone. This morning was no different.

It's oh-so-hard to be hopeful and grateful with a rumbling, grumbling stomach. The year was 1972, in a tiny apartment in Lynchburg, Virginia. A little family was scraping and clawing to survive. The husband was in his early twenties, a full-time, struggling college student while also a full-time auto mechanic trying to put food on his family's linoleum-top table. No matter how hard he worked, it was still a serious struggle to make ends meet. He and his young wife had a three-year-old son and another baby on the way. Across the previous week, they successfully stretched a single-pound of hamburger to last four meals—primarily sprinkled into a thin soup. One particular morning, they discovered the last loaf of bread had been eaten, and now the milk jug was dry. They even emptied the remaining dusty particles from the bottom of the Cheerios box. Before the man went out the door to class, they gave thanks and prayed for God's provision once again. Exasperated and feeling utterly defeated, he got into the family's old Ford, laid his head on the steering wheel, and cried out one more desperate prayer. He felt hungry, so alone, and just hoping for some help.

Playing with naming

Naomi certainly felt her own hunger and loneliness, radically surpassing the above-mentioned scenarios. She had experienced the bellyache hunger of famine and worse yet, deep heart-aching loss with the death of all three breadwinners in her life. By this point on our journey, you might be wondering, "Why is this ancient Hebrew account titled *Ruth*? It certainly seems like Naomi is the main character." Yes, Naomi is indeed the central character of the story. Layers of very deliberate literary technique were employed, an intentionality of text that highlights Naomi's all-out need and loneliness on her journey.

We previously noted the significance of characters' names in this story. Regarding that desperate summation statement of Ruth 1:5 and the reference to Naomi simply as "the woman/wife," Adele Berlin states:

> Here it is done for the emotional effect of the phrase—a woman stands alone: "The woman/wife remained without her two children and without her husband." She would, ordinarily, have lost all status now, but in our story she becomes a "mother-in-law." This is the only relationship that pertains; otherwise she stands independently, known only by her proper name. The way in

which Naomi is named confirms her centrality as a main character, and confirms the importance of the mother-in-law and daughter-in-law relationship.[1]

How other characters reference Naomi, her proper name's unique placement, and her status as mother-in-law—all play a vital role in how the story's readers perceive her.

Ironically, though she wanted to walk alone, though the two women likely traveled much of their remaining journey in silence, and though the story's literary artistry aims to demonstrate her emotional independence, Naomi was actually far from alone. Her ever-determined daughter-in-law insisted on joining the adventure back to Judah. Judy Fentress-Williams humorously observes the pivotal nature of this defining moment in the story:

> Ruth's decision to stay is the action upon which the rest of the narrative action hangs . . . It is what Oprah (not Orpah) calls the "aha!" moment. In Ruth, these "aha!" moments exist in the public sphere and in the unknown world . . . Here the women are severed from their geographic identity and their familial ties. In the absence of these all-important trappings of identity, Ruth makes a vow, a covenant, with Naomi. The vow that is made in secret is not only determinative for the action in that chapter but also for the entire narrative.[2]

Ruth demonstrated remarkable commitment, a ferocious devotion (Ruth 1:15–17). Most certainly, she had no way of knowing how her amazing emotional response toward her mother-in-law and the LORD would impact both short-term and long-term outcomes in the grand, redemptive story of God at work.

When they arrived, they were immediately surrounded by a buzz of excitement. The women of the village quickly gathered to cluck and chatter around Naomi, obviously stirred by the sudden arrival of this gone-so-long woman. "Can this be Naomi?" they exclaimed (Ruth 1:19). Ten plus years of strain and stress had not been kind to her countenance. In addition, their curiosity was

---

1. Berlin, *Poetics and Interpretation of Biblical Narrative*, 87.
2. Fentress-Williams, *Ruth*, 51.

kindled by the fact that three quarters of the family was missing—no husband and no sons were along.³

Naomi's response to their question reveals even more of her own mix of emotional turmoil. "Don't call me Naomi. Call me Mara, because the Almighty has made my life very bitter. I went away full, but the LORD has brought me back empty. Why call me Naomi? The LORD has afflicted me; the Almighty has brought misfortune upon me" (Ruth 1:20–21). What was she expressing? "Don't call me 'sweet and pleasant' (the meaning of Naomi). Instead, call me 'bitter' (the meaning of Mara). I left here full (at least with family around me), but now I'm coming back empty. I feel empty on multiple levels. Oh, and in case you're wondering *why*, let me tell you. The one who claims to be Almighty—in control as 'the King'—*he* is to blame."

> Ruth demonstrated remarkable commitment, a ferocious devotion. She had no way of knowing how her amazing emotional response toward her mother-in-law and the LORD would impact both short-term and long-term outcomes in the grand, redemptive story of God at work.

If you detect a few shades of sarcasm with her play on names and personal descriptors, your perception skills are right on target. John Tornfelt profoundly observes:

> Our God is not fragile. Our anger neither offends nor hurts Him. He is not so petty that He will smack us down for rudely speaking out against Him. But in verbalizing her feelings, Naomi was taking the first step on the road to recovery. She was starting to overcome the hurt. Naomi was putting into motion the emotions that she will need to get going again.⁴

Yes, as she was working out her bitterness in this conversation, she continued blaming God. It's a good thing for Naomi, and a very good thing for each of us—God is big enough emotionally to handle our blame games.

3. Sakenfeld, *Ruth*, 35.
4. Tornfelt, *Reunion*, 79.

Running on empty

Already running atrociously late for a meeting, I (JEP) was still forty-five minutes away. Zooming out Route 422, I stubbornly chose to ignore the gaslight. *Surely I can make it. After all, I think this tank's reserve runs about fifty miles.* I did not call my wife to ask how long the gas indicator light had been on. Within the half hour, while headed uphill, my van sputtered, stalled, and I coasted to the side of the road. I was in the middle of Nowheresville. Not only was I out of gas, I suddenly felt very, very alone. The summer day temperature was ninety-five degrees. I began walking downhill.

To my surprise, I found an auto repair shop about a half-mile back. The owner saw me walking down the road. He smiled as I walked in the door and just pointed to the front corner near the garage door. There sat an already-filled gas can. "'Happens several times a month," he chuckled. I smiled and told him I would bring the gas can back real soon, since my van was less than a mile back up Route 422. "Hold on, I'm due for a quick break." He laid down his wrench and wiped his greasy hands. "Let me grab keys and I'll run you up there." I thanked him profusely. My countenance changed, as I realized that in reality, I was far from alone.

Can you recall the last time you found yourself running on empty, feeling very alone in a financial crunch, and saying, "The LORD has afflicted me; the Almighty has brought misfortune upon me." Inside, you feel so hollow. Consider these scenarios where we often feel the financial crunch:

- You have a stack of unpaid bills sitting on the corner of the desk for the fourth month in a row. And the creditor calls have begun.
- Maybe you took the big leap to expand the business last year. It seemed like a smart move, a well-calculated risk at the time. You even prayed over the decision, but now, the money is just not there to sustain such expansion.
- Or perhaps you were forced to downsize your staff. Whereas you had sixty-five employees a decade ago, today you struggle

to keep fifteen on the payroll. And you've taken no personal cost-of-living increase during the previous three years in order to retain your team.

- You made the intentional budgeting decision five months ago: Start to regularly save PLUS truly tithe toward God's kingdom work. The first couple months seemed to go great, but over the past three months, resources were squeezed tighter and you have felt these commitments being tested more than ever.

- Maybe your kids have outgrown everything in their closets, and you wonder where you will find funds to buy at least a few new school clothes.

- Or you've discovered at least two different colors of fluid now dripping on your driveway. The twelve-year-old jalopy has already been in the shop four times in the past three months.

- Perhaps you've lost several loved ones, so near and dear, and they were also a major source of your sustenance.

One or more of these financial crunch scenarios, or something similar in nature has left you saying, "You cut me deep, Lord. You cut me real deep. And I feel so alone." How do you manage?

Fuel for flourishing

How do we survive financially, spiritually, and emotionally in the face of a financial crunch? God wonderfully intends for us to do more than just survive. The marvelous intentionality of God's original design, along with our being created in his image, included our call to "be fruitful, increase . . . fill the earth and subdue it. Rule over the fish in the sea and the birds in the sky and over every living creature." Such royal work and mission from God, often called the "cultural mandate," included the down-to-earth, daily bread reminder that God is the one who supplies the plants, trees, and seeds for humans and animals as food (Gen 1:28–30). Brian Fikkert and Russell Mask highlight this important insight:

Note that while God made the world "perfect," he left it "incomplete." This means that while the world was created to be without defect, God *called* humans to interact with creation, to make possibilities into realities, and to be able to sustain ourselves via the fruits of stewardship. In summary, when our entire substance—mind, heart, actions, and body—is living in right relationship to God, self, others, and the rest of creation, we experience *human flourishing*. This is what humans are created to be. It is the good life for which we are longing.[5]

Reality check. Our lives often feel very bad instead of good. In the wake of the Fall (Gen 3), humans' lives are extra-complicated, broken, and all too often, we feel like we are far from flourishing. We feel the pain, the distance, and the overall dark condition of our fallen existence. We do not experience those right relationships with God, self, others, and the rest of creation. Instead, we scrape and struggle to fulfill that original royal calling, to be fruitful leaders and flourish with creative productivity.

God is passionate for people to experience his transformation process, to be conformed once again to the image of Christ for the sake of others. When we humbly align our lives with God's will, his plans and processes, we can thrive in ways that are life-giving in multiple dimensions—in our emotional growth, personal skill development, relationships with others, faith/wisdom cultivation, and financial profit.

So how can we start to thrive and flourish in ways that are emotionally responsible and growth-oriented?

Such royal work and mission from God, often called the "cultural mandate," included the down-to-earth, daily bread reminder that God is the one who supplies the plants, trees, and seeds for humans and animals as food (Gen 1:28–30).

Three core perspectives can serve as life-giving fuel sources. When properly poured into our deepest places of need, they will empower us toward surviving, thriving, and flourishing for the sake of others.

---

5. Fikkert and Mask, *From Dependence to Dignity*, 82.

Here is our first fresh fuel source, a core perspective for filling up and flourishing: *Recognize God's primary, leading role, even when you can't yet fully see how he will provide.*

Ironically, though Naomi was still feeling her grievous loss and placing the blame for her dreadful misfortunes on the Almighty, she could not help but recognize his central, leading role in bringing her back. Tucked in her soulful complaint is this statement: "the LORD has brought me back" (Ruth 1:21). Katharine Sakenfeld observes:

> Naomi states that it is God who brought her back. In verse 6, the decision to return was described as Naomi's. Here as she speaks of her return as God's action, action in which she now sees nothing but sorrow, Naomi unknowingly anticipates the ways in which God will continue to work behind the scenes for the redemption of her tragedy.[6]

Be it ever so subtle, we can open our hearts to healthier progress when we acknowledge God's action, his vital role in sustaining us through tragic life events—even when we have not yet fully tasted his redemptive provision. We can anticipate something more with substantive hope, because the LORD himself supplies our fuel to thrive.

Our second source for filling up and flourishing is *truly valuing and depending on the friends God places on our paths.* Ironically, Naomi made no mention of Ruth as she conversed with the women of the village. Ruth was present, but she stood in the shadows as Naomi's tag-along, a stranger. Apparently, Naomi's grief was still running so deep, she struggled to fully see and appreciate Ruth. She remained consumed in her own loss. However, the storyteller makes sure *we* do not forget the vital role Ruth is playing. "So Naomi returned from Moab accompanied by Ruth the Moabite, her daughter-in-law" (Ruth 1:22). E. John Hamlin notes,

> Naomi did not yet know that God's answer to her cries was in the Moabite woman who had clung to her and

---

6. Sakenfeld, *Ruth*, 36.

sworn to walk by her side on her return to Bethlehem
... She would fill the void of emptiness in Naomi's heart
with fullness, embody God's grace instead of harshness, and bring blessing in place of calamity. She would
bring "hope for your future" (Jer 31:17), and change her
"mourning into dancing" (Ps 30:11).[7]

Though we each like to think we can go it alone, fly solo, and thrive as independent and self-sustaining agents, we actually need to join Naomi's gradually unfolding, down-to-earth epiphany: *we need others for friendship, support, and encouragement!* Batman had Robin. The Lone Ranger had Tonto. Don't forget, Shrek had Donkey. Though we may not like it, we may not readily realize it, and we may instinctively pull back like turtles into our self-protective shells, every one of us needs serious friendships for encouragement, support, and mutual resourcing on the journey.

Ugly battles but faithful friendships

The first day of the Battle of Shiloh was horrific. April 6, 1862. It was the bloodiest, deadliest day so far in this terrible War Between the States. Bruce Catton describes the aftermath of day one.

> It was a dreadful night. Toward midnight there was a hard thunderstorm, with a downpour to soak the soldiers who slept among the dead and wounded. Sudden flashes of lightning illuminated hideous scenes—dead men everywhere, pools and creeks given a ghastly tint by the blood of wounded men who crawled down to drink and had died with their faces in the water, brambly fields carpeted with torn bodies, helpless wounded men lying in the downpour chanting weak calls for help.[8]

Brigadier General William Tecumseh Sherman approached the man standing alone under a tree. Rain dripped off the man's hat brim. He had been injured by a fall from a horse a few days earlier

---

7. Hamlin, *Surely There Is a Future*, 23.
8. Catton, *Terrible Swift Sword*, 236.

and was now leaning on a crutch. With a lantern in his hand, he stared across the nightmarish scene. The losses for Major General Ulysses S. Grant and his men were devastating. At dawn, Grant's command had numbered thirty-seven thousand. By day's end, approximately seven thousand of those men were killed or wounded, and more than three thousand others were captured.

Sherman was a few years older than Grant, but Grant outranked him. In the shadows of the lantern's light, Sherman approached Grant in hopes of convincing his superior officer to evacuate their Union forces. Sherman believed such a pullback would be strategic in order to preempt any further damage by the Confederates.

Sherman respected and admired the younger Grant. They had many things in common. Both men were born in Ohio. Both loved their wives and adored their children. Grant and Sherman had spent extended periods of time in the South, and they loved the region and its people. Each of them was a graduate of the United States Military Academy at West Point. They knew the emotional turmoil of fighting against an enemy who was led by many of their close friends, schoolmates, and former military cohorts. One of the Confederate officers, James Longstreet, had been Grant's best man and was his cousin by marriage.

Grant and Sherman both knew the heartache of repeated failures. Not only had each man faced professional stumbles in civilian life, now each had been attacked by the press. Like most leaders, they had personal issues to conquer. One had been labeled a drunkard and the other vilified as insane. Such gross accusations were overstatements, mud slung by jealous officers who were vying for rank and prestige.

Along the way, these two war-scared generals had been learning to trust and communicate effectively with each other. In retrospect, people have called it their "magnetic telegraph." Often their headquarters were hundreds of miles apart but somehow, in an age devoid of cell phones, text messages or e-mails, they managed to remain in virtually constant contact. Each man consistently supported the other's efforts in every way possible.

On this night, as Sherman found Grant alone, he looked deeply into Grant's face and deciphered the determined expression. Sherman followed his wise instincts, and he suddenly decided not to mention retreat. He used a quiet, tentative approach. "Well, Grant," he said, "We've had the devil's own day of it, haven't we?" "Yes," Grant said. "Lick 'em tomorrow though."

The following day, Shiloh became a decisive Union victory. That meeting in the rain between Sherman and Grant symbolized yet another victory. Enormous results for the country flowed because a strong friendship and skillful communication formed between the two men. Some current historians believe it may be this friendship that won the Civil War.[9]

Ruth and Naomi, though weary and tattered by their own physical and emotional battles, were beginning to experience a similar, growing, and healthy interdependence. Their emerging interconnectedness would prove instrumental in the face of their hunger and deep feelings of hopeless loneliness. Though still unseen in the fog of the immediate financial-emotional crunch, this same fuel of friendship would prove to be redemptive, amazingly blessing others for generations to come.

Elephants for totems

Our third source of conceptual fuel, capable of filling up our empty condition and heading us toward flourishing, involves this hands-on action: *Pick up totems—tangible symbols—reminders of God's faithful promises to provide.*

I (JEP) have an intriguing totem—actually a set—sitting on the shelf behind my desk. They are a uniquely carved pair of elephants that I successfully bartered for and purchased from a Chinese merchant on a dusty backstreet in Hong Kong. I only paid a few dollars, but their real value is priceless.

The year was 1990. I was a college student with very little money, but I had sensed God wanted me to go global and learn

---

9. Flood, *Grant and Sherman*, 1–55.

some bigger mission principles. The trip's cost for nearly a month's stay would be fifteen hundred dollars. Yes, that would be an astounding deal for such a trip today, but it was an enormous sum of money for a twenty year old in that era.

I took the risk, signed up for the trip, and I had no real clue from where the resources would emerge. I'd like to say I was full of faith, but honestly, I was all over the map emotionally and at times very anxious. I prayed passionately and wondered. I paced my dorm room, calling on God to supply. My anxiety rose, but so did my prayers and my hopeful anticipation. I shared with people about my upcoming trip and asked for their help, steps that proved both humbling and formative. Marvelously, the Lord was faithful, supplying every penny of the fifteen hundred dollars.

My experiences on that trip proved profoundly transformative, supplying some of my earliest perspective shifts on God's link between entrepreneurial businesses, new churches, and God's expanding kingdom. Today, the carved elephants serve as totems, a constant reminder that God is big enough, and he faithfully provides. All these years later, when I am feeling a current financial crunch or a challenge of any size—sometimes for fifteen hundred dollars again, or at times hundreds of thousands for some new missional endeavor—I look at the elephants. I still get worked up, and I pace, and I call out to God, but my elephant totems are a constant, tangible reminder of how good, strong, and faithful the Almighty is to supply.

> That trip proved profoundly transformative, supplying some of my earliest perspective shifts on God's link between entrepreneurial businesses, new churches, and God's expanding kingdom. Today, the carved elephants serve as totems, a constant reminder that God is big enough, and he faithfully provides.

As they returned, Naomi and Ruth had two totems to greet them. The town itself was a huge totem. *Bethlehem.* This town's name literally means "house of bread."[10] Though they had experienced the severe season of famine, this little town's name served as a constant reminder of God's

10. Sasson, *Ruth*, 15.

faithfulness to sustain and supply for his people. And there would come a far-off day in the distant future when this place, House of Bread, would serve as the birthplace for a boy who would satisfy humanity's deepest hunger and ultimately supply the greatest hope for flourishing. (But now we're jumping way ahead in the story.)

In addition, Naomi and Ruth had one other oh-so-tangible totem. The storyteller reports that they arrived in Bethlehem "as the barley harvest was beginning" (Ruth 1:22). The sheaves of barley were waving at them from the fields. What a substantial, visual reminder of God's faithfulness. The scenery all around them screamed the message, "God is faithful. He provides."

For your own fresh source of conceptual fuel, pause and soak up these hope-filled promises of God's resources, capable of filling us up and leading us toward flourishing. The psalmist gave praise: "The eyes of all look to you, and you give them their food at the proper time. You open your hand and satisfy the desires of every living thing" (Ps 145:15–16). Centuries later, the Apostle Paul explained to the believers at Philippi: "I have received full payment and have more than enough. I am amply supplied, now that I have received from Epaphroditus the gifts you sent . . . And my God will meet all your needs according to the riches of his glory in Christ Jesus" (Phil 4:18–19). Such precious promises fill us with Christ-focused, others-oriented hope, capable of carrying us through any financial crunch we might face.

Back to Buffalo . . . and to Lynchburg

Still a half-mile from school, the young boy thrust his hands deeper and plunged ahead through the snow. He suddenly discovered that each pocket of his tattered coat contained a piping-hot, foil-wrapped potato. His mother's dual purpose proved brilliant—warm hands now and something to fill his belly at lunchtime. In spite of what seemed like meager resources and though this was the daily menu for lunch and many other meals for over five years of the Great Depression, the boy's family faithfully said grace each evening. They deliberately thanked the good Lord for his blessings.

Against all odds, the young man's family survived and even learned to flourish with daily doses of joyful gratitude.

This young boy of Depression-era Buffalo was Holly's father and John's grandfather, Everett C. Hall. He told the story often while Holly was growing up and then again when John was a young lad. As a result, when Holly and Kenny, the twenty-something couple going to college in Virginia, found themselves wondering and praying for more bread and milk, they remembered the family story from four decades back, a story of God's faithful provision. As Kenny lifted his head from praying over the steering wheel that morning, he spied two dimes jammed between the old Ford's dash and windshield. Back in the early 1970s, a dime bought a loaf of bread and another dime would buy a pint of milk. They had no recollection of ever sticking dimes on that dash, but the young couple readily recognized that someone's hand stuck them there. Later the same day, there was an envelope in his college mailbox with fifty dollars cash—entirely anonymous. Such enormous provision would supply two weeks' worth of groceries for the hungry but now full family.

Two potatoes, two dimes, two carved elephants, Bethlehem and a barley harvest—they serve as constant reminders that in even the most ferocious financial crunch, God is faithful to provide. Such tangible totems, the supportive friends whom God places on our paths, and his very own leading role, ever-present in the center of our circumstances—these are ample, rich resources to fuel our journey.

Our story is far from over. On the next leg of the adventure, we will walk forward and more fully consider one of the most unique arenas where our emotions get pressure-tested. Everyday, in the rough and tumble of our workplaces, how can we tap into stronger emotional resources for ongoing flourishing?

Questions for reflection and discussion

1. When have you personally, your business, or your family experienced a financial crunch? Describe how you felt.

2. How does Naomi and Ruth's story reflect a financial crunch? What are the indicators that they were running on empty?

3. What do you think about God's intention for human flourishing (Gen 1:28-30) and the importance of people living in right relationship to God, self, others, and the rest of creation? Is such flourishing truly possible today, or nearly impossible? Why?

4. How can our recognition of God's leading role in our story—even when we don't yet fully see his provision—supply us with the start of fresh hope?

5. When have you seen faithful friendships prove vital in your own life battles, financial crunches, and other emotional struggles?

6. What might serve as your own totems, those tangible symbols reminding you of God's faithfulness to provide?

7. How are Psalm 145:15–16 and Philippians 4:18–19 helpful in affirming and growing your faith during this current season?

CHAPTER FIVE

Hard 'n Hearty Work

Opportunity is missed by most people because it's dressed in overalls and looks like work.

—EDISON

Born in 1907, Earl grew up in rural New England. His mother took in laundry, and his father was described as a friendly tinkerer who lacked ambition and whose farming businesses never succeeded. Young Earl, however, had little patience with his father's lack of drive. Although not much of a student, he was enterprising from an early age. When he was ten years old, he started his first business, selling the family produce door to door. His favorite pastime was inventing things, and he kept a detailed notebook of his latest inventions. Earl persistently tried to sell his ideas but had little luck. After high school graduation, he took a course in advertising but still was not able to market his inventions with any success.

Earl Tupper married Marie Whitcomb in 1931, and they had five children. He started Tupper's Tree Surgery and Landscaping but was forced into bankruptcy during the Depression. With a family to provide for, Earl felt very fortunate to get a job in the Viscaloid plastic factory, a division of DuPont. On the side, he managed to buy himself a few used molding machines and began experimenting. Just after World War II, Tupper asked DuPont for some pure polyethylene pellets so he could try molding some practical peacetime plastic products. DuPont agreed to let him try. Tupper was tenacious, and after many trials and errors, he produced the first Tupperware bowl. Eventually, his Wonderbowl made it into department stores and even won some design prizes. However, in spite of such early inroads, his product was not meeting with strong sales success and appeared to be tanking, just like his earlier dream products.[1]

Whatever our field of work—a hospital room or boardroom, stock market or supermarket—each workplace produces its share of stress, risks, fears, relational turmoil, potential pitfalls, and overall tests of character. With such forces at work on our souls, our emotions play a pivotal role. Out of control, mismanaged, or underdeveloped, desperate emotions prove overwhelming. Elizabeth Johnston and Leah Olson warn:

> Anxiety disorders, which include phobias, panic attacks, posttraumatic stress disorder (PTSD), obsessive-compulsive disorder, and generalized anxiety disorder, are among the most common and debilitating . . . They interfere with day-to-day functioning in the schoolroom, workplace, and social sphere, and bring with them significant health outcomes, including risk of depression and substance abuse.[2]

How we choose to respond, our deeper choices when processing such emotional challenges, will prove pivotal in determining whether or not we experience personal transformation that leads to greater flourishing, both for ourselves and for others.

Mishandled emotions can lead to bungled relational scenarios, lousy teamwork, and an overall loss of bottom line productivity and revenue. Consider it. The sheer volume of hours we spend on our daily tasks creates the potential for either great failure or immense personal growth. Hence, the workplace is an astoundingly important arena for our emotional development.

---

1. "Tupperware: About the Film," http://www.pbs.org/wgbh/americanexperience/features/biography/tupperware-tupper/

2. Johnston and Olson, *The Feeling Brain*, 65–66.

Dusty bags and the bachelor

On the journey back to Bethlehem, Naomi and Ruth carried their share of heavy emotional baggage, including feelings of apprehension, emptiness, disappointment, and likely indicators of dismal depression in the wake of their tragic losses. Naomi revealed layers of complex, deeper feelings as she spewed on Bethlehem's circle of women the reasons she preferred to be called *Mara*, "bitter" instead of her actual name, *Naomi*, which meant "sweet." We can sense toxic tension in her tone. During this conversation, Ruth was tucked in the shadows, virtually ignored by her mother-in-law.

While she had every reason to feel forgotten and overwhelmed—a weighty burden of grief, the stress of leaving home, the serious nature of her big commitment to both Naomi and God, a still-looming uncertainty of financial provision, plus numerous other unknowns regarding their future—Ruth actually demonstrated significant progress throughout this painful journey. Carolyn James makes this profound observation about the transformation in Ruth's life:

> Ruth is hurting too. But while she faces the same oppressive realities, she is being reshaped by the vow she pledged to Naomi on the journey. Her vow drives her actions and informs her choices from the moment she swears loyalty to Naomi until the day the younger widow dies. We will never understand Ruth if we leave her vow behind. By her own choice she will no longer think solely of herself or live in pursuit of personal happiness . . . Energized by her vow to Naomi and her newfound faith in Yahweh, Ruth turns outward and mobilizes.[3]

Ruth boldly owned her deep emotions, made big-league choices, and moved forward on her journey of personal spiritual formation for the sake of others.

Accompanying such progress in the face of her pain, Ruth carried some additional baggage the storyteller shoves front and center. At both the wrap-up of Ruth 1 and the launch of Ruth 2, she

---

3. James, *The Gospel of Ruth*, 94.

was deliberately labeled "the Moabite." Such status tells us that in the eyes of the people of Bethlehem, she initially appeared as the despised foreigner from that fiendish land of Moab. She was the stranger, a questionable outsider from an unholy land whose people caused previous conflict and supplied ongoing contrast to God's holy people of Judah.

As chapter 2 opens in Ruth's story, we are introduced to a brand new character, a relative on Naomi's husband's side, "a man of standing from the clan of Elimelek." His name was Boaz (Ruth 2:1). Such early description of this individual is packed with purpose, revealing the man's overall sterling character and stellar life status. While current-day readers might fancifully imagine a stunningly good looking, Judeo-Christian version of *the Bachelor*, we can't be certain how tall, dark, and handsome Boaz truly was. Even his current marital status remains mysterious. What we *are* given is an overall character reference. "A man of standing" identifies him as a seriously noble leader in the eyes of others, a man of significant influence and prominence.

> We can encounter more productive methods of working through our own rough and tumble of workplace emotions. Could such work actually match God's transformative purpose in our lives, leading us to be even more conformed to the image of Christ for the sake of others?

His name, *Boaz*, means "in strength." We dare not miss it. With such strong integrity, he stood head and shoulders above others in his day—especially when you recall that our story happened in that stormy stretch of years, when "every man did whatever was right in his own eyes" (Judg 21:25). Boaz was an impressively influential individual in the community who stood out like a diamond on display against a jet-black backdrop.

Such description serves to pique our curiosity and prompts us to wonder. Perhaps this man will help these struggling women. And perhaps with his outstanding example, we can encounter more productive methods of working through our own rough and tumble of workplace emotions. Could such work actually match

God's transformative purpose in our lives, leading us to be even more conformed to the image of Christ for the sake of others? In the story's next scenes, we encounter fresh conversations and discover how to cultivate emotionally healthy leadership in and through our workplaces. As we engage these conversations, we will discover a handful of healthy postures for becoming seriously strong, emotionally intelligent workplace leaders.

Thumbs up for good old-fashioned hard work

The tale is told of a company in Oslo, Norway, that was weary of placing HELP WANTED ads and receiving very few applicants. Determined to get better results, they creatively posted: "Tiresome and boring wholesale company seeks indolent people with a total lack of service-mindedness for a job that is completely without challenge. If you're still interested, sit down. Have a cup of coffee. Relax. If you can be bothered, give us a call." Over one hundred thirty people called—far more than when the company ran ads for hard-working, super-motivated, friendly employees. Sadly, such a response is indicative of pervasive outlooks regarding good old-fashioned hard work.

Immediately following the storyteller's character description of Boaz (vs. 1), Ruth asked Naomi's permission to go pick up leftover barley in the fields, following the regular harvest workers. Naomi gave the go-ahead, so Ruth set out, entered a field, and began to glean behind the harvesters. Ruth demonstrated our first foundational and crucial posture of emotionally tuned-in leaders. She held an extremely positive perspective on good, hard work. The Theology of Work Project shares a snapshot synopsis of the whole scene:

> Ruth was eager to work hard to support herself and Naomi. "Let me go to the field," she implored, and when she was given a chance to work, her co-workers reported that "she has been on her feet from early this morning until now, without resting even for a moment" (Ruth 2:7). Her work was exceptionally productive. When she

came home after her first day at work and beat out the barley from the stalks, her harvest yielded a full ephah of grain (Ruth 2:17) . . . Both God and Boaz commended (and rewarded) her for her faith and industry (Ruth 2:12, 17–23; 3:15–18).[4]

Ruth's efforts reveal a motivated outlook. *Bring it on—I'm eager to work!* She was not adverse to entering a field and pouring her whole self into a hard day's labor.

So often, we allow a negative view of work to sneak into our emotions and resulting actions. We feel like *work is such a pain! What a horrific curse! If I could just win the lottery or land a lucky break, then my life would be complete.* Or we say to ourselves, *I'd have real significance if I had my dream job.* And many of us privately emote: *I just have to trudge through the drudgery of my week, and I can't wait for the weekend.*

We might forget that we first encounter God as the ultimate creator/worker (Gen 1). Shaped in his likeness, we were designed to bear his image (Gen 1:26–28), including that kingdom work that led to a flourishing garden (Gen 2:15). And though sin's curse had a negative effect on all creation, including human work and our emotions about labor (Gen 3:17–19), a grand reverse of the curse is included in God's redemptive plans (Rom 8:18–25). Such a reversal must also include the original ideals of God-like labor, wholesome attitudes, and productive outcomes of such kingdom work.

Bill Peel and Walt Larimore affirm: "God is a worker. Unlike gods of Greek and Eastern thought, the God of the Bible is actively involved in every aspect of His world. He rolled up His sleeves, so to speak, as He engaged in creation. The words *physical* and *earthy* describe God's work of creation."[5] In spite of our too-often negative emotions toward good old-fashioned, hands-on labor, the whole of God's story, from cover to cover, portrays an overall positive view of work.

---

4. Theology of Work Project, http://www.theologyofwork.org/old-testament/ruth-and-work.

5. Peel and Larimore, *Workplace Grace*, 36.

Jesus was and is a worker. When we work "in the name of the Lord Jesus" (Col 3:17), reflecting his character in our endeavors, we actually join Christ at work. Eugene Peterson connects the dots:

> Twenty-seven times in John's Gospel, Jesus is identified as a worker: "My Father is still working, and I also am working" (John 5:17). Work doesn't take us away from God; it continues the work of God. We observe that God comes into view on the first page of our Scripture as a worker, creating the universe. Once we identify God in his workplace working, it isn't long before we find ourselves in our workplaces working in the name of God.[6]

We glean meaningful work motivation from Christ, and we dare not miss Ruth's exemplary attitude and actions. Her proactive and productive labor in the barley field demonstrated a God-honoring, pro-work posture.

Wonder women at work

Earl Tupper felt confident that he had an innovative product. Nevertheless, sales were flat-lined and fumbling, despite its availability in select department stores.[7] Remarkably, that all changed when Tupper, the reclusive, introverted, eccentric perfectionist met and hired a flamboyant, extroverted, energy-charged woman.

Brownie Wise was a divorced single parent—in a time when divorce was still taboo and single motherhood was certainly not the norm. Wise had no formal business training and minimal sales experience. For several years, she supported herself, her son, and her mother by working as a secretary. There were few lucrative career opportunities available for women in the 1940s and 50s. Brownie began selling Stanley Home Products door to door shortly after World War II. When her son became very ill in 1949, she followed the doctor's advice and moved her little family to Florida.

---

6. Peterson, in his Foreword to Stevens and Ung's *Taking Your Soul to Work*, ix.

7. Kealing, *Tupperware Unsealed*, 23.

With her mother's help, she developed a social network and sold a variety of household products at home patio parties. Some of the most popular products sold at Brownie's parties were Earl Tupper's plastic Wonderbowls.

Wise came to Tupper's attention because of her high volume of Tupperware sales. He was still searching for a profitable outlet for his plastic containers. In 1951, Tupper met with Brownie Wise and discussed the development of a home party plan as a way to sell his company's products. He took a gigantic risk and decided to hire this dynamic, ambitious, capable woman as vice president of the Tupperware Home Parties.[8] Tupperware would now be sold *exclusively* through the home party system.

During the next few years, Brownie Wise built the Tupperware Home Party plan. Focused on recruitment efforts of women and their established social networks, she developed an innovative system of sales and recruitment incentives. Brownie became famous for elaborate awards ceremonies and generous gifts to top company dealers and distributors. Her success was lauded by the sales industry, and women idolized her. She was a constant favorite for women's magazine articles. In 1954, Wise was the first woman to appear on the cover of Business Week magazine as the leader of a multi-million dollar corporation.

> Jesus was and is a worker. When we work "in the name of the Lord Jesus" (Col 3:17), reflecting his character in our endeavors, we actually join Christ at work.

After arriving in ancient Bethlehem, Naomi and Ruth could have claimed they were simply praying, waiting, and trusting God to cover their needs. As we've already seen, their faith in God had deepened through the dark storms, but theirs was far from a passive faith. Ruth did not simply fold her hands in petition for provision. She strategized, planned, and set her hands to work in the sheaves.

A robust, God-like perspective on work shakes off any hint of passive slouch that's couched in a veneer of faith or some lazy

---

8. Ibid., 52-53.

hopes that bank on the latest get-rich-quick scheme. Instead, with all our heart, soul, and strength—yes, *Shema*-style, the epitome of enthusiastic emotions—we choose to give hard work a big attitudinal thumbs-up. Just like both Ruth and Brownie, we can embrace hard work with joyful energy and passionate panache.

Skillful communication—creating dynamic teamwork!

Ruth began working in a field belonging to Boaz, and when Boaz arrived, his interaction with the harvesters indicated an amazingly healthy level of communication as well as the marvelous corporate culture of his business. Boaz greeted his team with gregarious words of God-focused blessing, and their response was warmly reciprocal (Ruth 2:4). Boaz was curious and asked the harvest overseer regarding this mysterious woman who had arrived. The overseer's answer denotes that there had been a strong transference of Boaz' faith-filled values to his team of leaders (Ruth 2:6–7). Apparently, Boaz had taught and modeled such values, and his work team had caught them. Ruth obviously received the green light to glean, revealing the work team's serious commitment to share in God's care for the poor. Boaz' team had been well-trained in advance, and they were all on the same page, passionately owning a set of shared values that showed up in living color on that day Ruth arrived.

Through Boaz' immediate and responsive interaction with Ruth, he demonstrated sensitive and decisive communication skills. Remember, for Ruth and everyone working in the field, this was hard, serious, hands-on labor. Again, we must do our best to clear away all those wispy, romantic notions of a gorgeously made-up, hair-curled, sweet-smelling heroine meeting *the Bachelor* for the first time. Instead, Boaz greeted a grimy, windblown, garbed-for-gleaning, feisty woman, covered in barley dust. No doubt, he indeed thought she looked hot, but not exclusively with our current-day connotation of attraction. She was most definitely gleaming and glistening—probably with profuse sweat.

Modeling remarkable kindness, clarity, and intentionality, Boaz supplied caring conversation and positive affirmation. His harvest workday included breaks for water, refreshment, and a generous lunch—not just for Ruth but his whole team. We observe a positive ethos in their overall harvest culture, very intentionally cultivated by Boaz' thoughtful, leading communication.

Back in Tupperware world, trouble was brewing, and by 1958 it would eventually boil over. Initially, Tupper and Wise worked well together in spite of their obvious personality differences, unique approaches to business, and varied communication skills. Tupper was happy to remain in Massachusetts overseeing the creation of all new products at the corporation. He was a hovering, hands-on leader who needed his input and skills to be a part of all designs and processes. Wise thoroughly enjoyed leading the Tupperware Home Party division from its Florida base.

While Earl personally shunned public exposure, national recognition came with the phenomenal success of the company, and Brownie Wise's public role grew in prominence. In the early days, Tupper and Wise communicated effectively through long phone calls and extensive memos, but by 1957 the lines of communication were breaking down. Soon, the two were clashing frequently over management and direction of the business. Some individuals inside the inventor's closest circle believe he became jealous of all the recognition Brownie received.

Tupper grew painfully paranoid. He seemed consumed by the idea that Wise was plotting a corporate takeover of the company. Wise wrote and published a book about her life and success. Tupper was infuriated when she failed to allow him to read and evaluate it before publication. He became enraged over a photo of Brownie's dog eating from a Tupperware bowl. Both the photo and Tupper's emotions flew public. Wise simply shrugged it off as ridiculous. Over the next months, they continued to clash. When they did meet face to face, they were confrontational, and Wise showed only minimal respect

---
Proactive communication skills make a remarkable posture for productive teamwork.

Hard 'n Hearty Work

toward Tupper and his leadership. The differences that had made their original work efforts such a phenomenal success were now tearing them apart. Clearly, neither of them understood how to successfully work through their gaping distance in emotional makeup, communication style, and personality differences.

One day in January 1958, Earl Tupper uncharacteristically showed up in Florida and announced a special meeting. Not present at the meeting was Brownie Wise. Tupper definitively declared to two of his top executives, Gary McDonald and Hamer Wilson, Brownie Wise was finished as vice president of Tupperware Home Parties and would be fired that same day. McDonald and Wilson were shocked and surprised to learn that Tupper was looking to them to lead the company through the transition and into the future.[9]

Naturally, Brownie Wise was taken by surprise. She sued the company and later settled out of court for about $30,000. She received no stock in the company she had worked so hard to promote to world recognition. Undaunted, Wise went on to found three other direct sales companies. She remained in Florida and was highly respected and well-liked by all who knew her. She died in 1992 at the age of 79.

Much of what Boaz modeled so well (and Tupper struggled to employ with crucial team members) is what Daniel Goleman calls primal leadership. He explains:

> How easily we catch leaders' emotional states, then, has to do with how expressively their faces, voices and gestures convey their feelings. The greater a leader's skill at transmitting emotions, the more forcefully the emotions will spread. Such transmission does not depend on theatrics ... If you think about the leaders with whom people most want to work in an organization, they probably have this ability to exude upbeat feelings. It's one reason emotionally intelligent leaders attract talented people—for the pleasure of working in their presence. Conversely, leaders who emit the negative register—who

---

9. Kealing, *Tupperware Unsealed*, 188-197.

are irritable, touchy, domineering, cold—repel people. No one wants to work for a grouch.[10]

Recognizing such a vital role of leaders in establishing a business' culture, Goleman calls us to passionate communication and implementation of bright emotional intelligence with our work teams.

Spotlighting a corporate team in Malaysia, Goleman masterfully articulates a synopsis of such resonant leadership. He describes the remarkable changes and increased productivity that transpired for that group of leaders. Their business endeavor had previously been desperately struggling to survive and thrive. However, their turn-around proved tremendous. Goleman queries:

> What had happened? The same people were there; personnel hadn't changed much during that time. What had changed was how they worked together: The climate became one that encouraged everyone to increase their use of emotional intelligence and to build their leadership talent. Each manager had the opportunity to articulate his dreams and aspirations . . . to see himself as others saw him through 360-degree feedback . . . to develop a personal learning agenda . . . and to experiment and practice new habits of leadership at work . . . They developed emotional resonance about their mission and development as leaders.[11]

Whether it's the life-giving resonance of Boaz' team, the fumbling communication demonstrated by mid-twentieth-century Tupper and Wise, or Malaysian leaders and their team's experiencing a fantastic shift in corporate culture, this much is certain. Proactive communication skills make a remarkable posture for productive teamwork.

---

10. Goleman, *Primal Leadership*, 11–12.
11. Ibid., 167–168.

Hard 'n Hearty Work
Laser-focused, passionate mission to bless others

Great communication is vital for leaders and their workplaces if they are going to be emotionally healthy and flourishing. In a foundational way, a positive view of creative, God-honoring work must permeate the business. But what lies beneath? What posture undergirds and supplies the substantial content of such resonant leadership's positive outlook and team-oriented communication? For Christ-honoring, emotionally savvy workplaces, there's a passionate commitment to God's deep, over-arching, and far-reaching mission. Boaz' interaction with the harvesters carried the rich language of *blessing*. "The LORD be with you," was Boaz' greeting. "The LORD bless you!" they answered (Ruth 2:4b). Later in the chapter, when Naomi saw the productive results and heard the details of Ruth's workday, she employed the same *blessing* language regarding Boaz. "The LORD bless him" (Ruth 2:20).

This blessing concept was far more significant than our current day's quick blessings when people sneeze or say bedtime prayers. Boaz' greeting meant so much more than "best wishes" or "may the force be with you." With great intentionality, these characters were echoing rich concepts from their long-term faith story. God's blessing emerged in the opening of God's story when he purposefully blessed humans (Gen 1:28). Such a blessing was part and parcel of God's intentions that his

> For Christ-honoring, emotionally savvy workplaces, there's a passionate commitment to God's deep, over-arching, and far-reaching mission.

creation, his kingdom, and his kingdom leaders would flourish. Following the fall, the curse, and the ongoing dismal outcomes (Gen 3–11), God called Abram to go to a new land and "be a blessing." God's long-range aim was that all the nations—people groups, tribes, and families all over the earth—would "be blessed" through Abram's faith-filled life (Gen 12:1–3). This is what the Apostle Paul called "the Gospel in advance" (Gal 3:6–9)—in a certain sense, God's first installment of the great commission—antecedent to

Christ's eventual commission for global disciple making (Matt 28:18–20).[12]

But what does such mission of blessing truly entail, and what might applications look like for our work today? First, Boaz worked to create *an exceptional workplace, committed to being ethical, fully honoring God.* He supplied strong directives to his workers about how Ruth should be treated with utmost respect in his field. Winsomely, the *Theology of Work Project* suggests this might be the world's earliest example of an anti-sexual harassment policy.[13] All descriptions of the workplace conditions and related conversations reveal that Boaz' business was a safe, supportive, and flourishing environment (Ruth 2:8–16). Such faithful, regular practices no doubt contributed to his outstanding reputation in the community (Ruth 2:1).

Jeff Van Duzer posits high ethics as the everyday expectation for every worker. He champions a set of practical behaviors reflecting God-glorifying excellence:

> At a minimum Christians in business should conduct themselves with integrity. They should insist on being law-abiding and seek to comply with all applicable company policies. They should be hard–working, giving an honest day's work for an honest day's wage. Christians should be kind and compassionate to co-workers, avoid gossip and be generous of spirit in dealing with others. To the extent it is up to them, they should conduct their business in a way that does not inflict harm on others. Christians should work for the best interest of their company and community rather than focusing just on their own personal advancement. They should be humble, good listeners and eager to learn. All of these traits and more honor God and can be put into practice regardless of one's status within the company.[14]

---

12. Wright, *The Mission of God*, 194–95; 247.

13. Theology of Work Project, http://www.theologyofwork.org/old-testament/ruth-and-work.

14. Van Duzer, *Why Business Matters*, 193.

Workplaces characterized by such commitment to God-glorifying ethics will faithfully fulfill their mission of blessing others.

Second, Boaz' business dealings included *very intentional efforts to follow God's passion and plans for alleviating poverty*. The agri-business work of gleaning—picking up leftovers, following after the harvesters—was not Boaz' dream scheme. These plans originated from God's directives. Catch the heart and detail of this Levitical instruction:

> When you reap the harvest of your land, do not reap to the very edges of your field or gather the gleanings of your harvest. Do not go over your vineyard a second time or pick up the grapes that have fallen. Leave them for the poor and the foreigner. I am the Lord your God (Lev 19:9–10).

And observe these Deuteronomic applications of God's compassion:

> When you are harvesting in your field and you overlook a sheaf, do not go back to get it. Leave it for the foreigner, the fatherless and the widow, so that the Lord your God may bless you in all the work of your hands. When you beat the olives from your trees, do not go over the branches a second time. Leave what remains for the foreigner, the fatherless and the widow. When you harvest the grapes in your vineyard, do not go over the vines again. Leave what remains for the foreigner, the fatherless and the widow. Remember that you were slaves in Egypt. That is why I command you to do this (Deut 24:19–22).

Such others-oriented commands went way beyond nice-sounding, pie-in-the-sky ideals for Boaz. He was deeply committed to leading his business according to divine directives of serving those less fortunate. It's stunning to remember that other business leaders of that era were doing "whatever seemed right in their own eyes." Boaz' obedience to God's commands reflected a passion for leading his business based on biblical direction, aiming to fully follow the Lord's heart for those in need.

When our family was living in rural Michigan in the early 1980s, we were struggling to survive, squeaking by on an extremely limited income. Deeply needy, we were constantly watching for God's supply. In those same years, we had a small hobby farm that included ten or more hogs and perhaps a dozen chickens. While we certainly enjoyed the animals for hobby and entertainment, they also served as an integral part of our family's food supply. Obviously, it takes grain to feed chickens and hogs, so as to gain eggs and bacon. Ground-up corn feed was pricey. On adjoining property lived a farmer, whose practice was to leave the four corners of his field unharvested, thus allowing needy families such as ours to come and glean. Amazingly, he was passionate about applying God's principles in his agri-business, taking his clues from Leviticus 23:22. "When you reap the harvest of your land, do not reap to the very edges of your field or gather the gleanings of your harvest. Leave them for the poor and for the foreigner residing among you. I am the Lord your God." With joyful gratitude, our family discussed the farmer's God-honoring correlation to present-day.

Each day after school in late September through early November of 1982, we worked like crazy in his field's corners. We were also allowed to walk throughout the entire rest of the field to pick up ears of corn that had been missed by the harvesting equipment. Once gathered, that supply of corn was then ground into feed. Remarkably, this feed carried us through much of the winter of 1983. I (JEP) recall my dad plucking ears of corn and measuring them across his arm. Some ears spanned from his elbow to his fingertips. Stunned by their size, he exclaimed, "These have to be some of the largest ears of corn I have ever seen." And with a gigantic grin, Dad proclaimed, "God certainly has blessed our farmer friend's faithfulness to follow God's principles."

Global emotions—going beyond charity

Here is a vitally important corollary concept we must consider, coinciding with God's passion and plans for poverty alleviation. Notice carefully Boaz' highly intentional and emotionally sensitive approach. Based on learning of Ruth and Naomi's condition, he could have taken a "give-a-hand-out," charity-based approach—free grain or free bread for these needy widows. Instead, he created a business culture that deliberately included workspace for those less fortunate, supplying ample room for them to work with dignity.

Brian Fikkert and Russell Mask declare a vital poverty alleviation principle layered with emotional responsibility: "Poverty alleviation is the ministry of reconciliation, seeking to restore poor people to what God created them to be. One result is that people will be able to glorify God through work and to support their families through that work."[15] Boaz' resonant leadership and his commitment to follow this harvest directive supplied Ruth with the work of gleaning and the resulting grain with which she could skillfully make bread. Hence, the entire business process not only supplied food but also preserved human dignity. Ruth was able to skillfully work, express the image of God in her, and actively fulfill her *hesed*-based, God-honoring vow.

With similar motivation, Wayne Grudem challenges today's business leaders to think more strategically and redemptively about their roles:

> How should we open our heart to our brother in need? A short-term solution is to give food and clothing to the poor, and that is certainly right. But it is no long-term solution, for the food is soon eaten and the clothing wears out. I believe the only long-term solution to world poverty is business. That is because businesses produce goods, and businesses produce jobs. And businesses continue producing goods year after year, and continue providing jobs and paying wages year after year. Therefore if we are ever going to see *long-term* solutions to world poverty, I believe it will come through starting and maintaining productive, profitable businesses.[16]

---

15. Fikkert and Mask, *From Dependence to Dignity*, 39.
16. Grudem, "How Business in Itself Can Glorify God," 150–151.

Grudem's vision for such business-based solutions to poverty motivates us to dream and strategize toward more long-term, life-saving, and life-changing endeavors.

Mimose is another wonder woman, working so hard and making marvelous impact. She lives in the Cadiac community, approximately two-and-a-half hours southwest of Port-Au-Prince in Haiti. Mimose owns a Coca-Cola business, a warehouse that supplies soda pop to numerous roadside merchants across the region. Her business is strong and profitable—in a region previously typified by deep poverty and rampant crime. How did such flourishing become a reality? Several years ago, a group of thoughtful leaders in her community, passionate to share God's blessings, began to dream, plan, and launch savings groups. In these intentionally small circles, people gather to learn holistic life skills, contribute resources together, cultivate Christ-focused discipleship, and eventually make loans to each other. Mimose started out as a member of an early savings group, developed in her faith, consistently saved money, and learned skills for blessing others through business. Now years later, she not only leads her growing Coke distribution business, but she also serves as a savings group leader, helping others who need to learn the same life-giving principles.[17]

Boaz was not content to engage in such blessing business as letter-of-the-law fulfillment. He aimed to show lavish loving kindness, the kind that would lead Ruth and Naomi to flourish. The *Theology of Work Project* notes:

> Boaz was inspired to go significantly beyond what the law required in providing for the poor and vulnerable. The gleaning laws merely required landowners to leave some produce in the fields for foreigners, orphans and widows to glean. This generally meant the poor and vulnerable had difficult, dangerous, uncomfortable work, such as harvesting grain at the weedy edges of fields or high up in olive trees. The produce they obtained this way was usually of inferior quality, such as grapes and olives that

---

17.. View additional stories of God's work in Haiti, via video captured on JEP's journeys in Haiti. Go to http://johneltonpletcher.com/work-stories-videos-from-haiti/.

had fallen to the ground or had not fully ripened. But Boaz tells his workers to be actively generous. They were to remove first-quality grain from the stalks they had cut, and leave them lying on top of the stubble so Ruth would need merely to pick them up. Boaz's concern was not to minimally fulfill a regulation, but to genuinely provide for Ruth and her family.[18]

Such creative examples can spark our entrepreneurial imaginations. How might we work with God to create more life-shaping, family-flourishing workplaces?

Emotionally responsible workplace leaders who are committed to the mission of blessing others intentionally choose exceptional, God-honoring ethics as the basis for each day's work. They engage such stellar ethics in both their tasks and their opportunities for relational interaction. In addition, they deliberately cultivate profitable business for greater job creation that leads to poverty alleviation marked by marvelous dignity. And the third very deliberate focus for blessing-focused workplace leaders is to *strategically express God's love to the outsiders—the foreigners, the marginalized, those previously outside the faith community.*

With such focus, we embrace God's global mission—to welcome and enfold more people. Boaz very intentionally lived out Leviticus 19:34: "The foreigner residing among you must be treated as your native-born. Love them as yourself, for you were foreigners in Egypt. I am the Lord your God." Pause to recall Ruth's label. She was readily known to Judah's inhabitants as "the Moabite."

> Create a business culture that deliberately includes workspace for those less fortunate, supplying ample room for people to work with dignity. Help restore people to what God created them to be—glorifying God and supporting their families through such robust work!

Here is the thick, loving thread of God's mission, to reach the nations, to intentionally include the outsiders, those from other people groups. Love for the foreigner is a

---

18. Theology of Work Project, http://www.theologyofwork.org/old-testament/ruth-and-work.

phenomenal method of applying the second greatest commandment, the others-oriented portion of your calling: "Love your neighbor as yourself" (Lev 19:18; Matt 22:39). Boaz was demonstrating the faithful life of a God-follower. In a real sense, he was a gospel-centered, mission-driven, disciple-making business owner. Boaz was consistently demonstrating to his workers how faithful God-followers reveal God's *hesed*-style love in their daily work.

Working with Jesus

We can glean correlating insights from another field of workers several centuries later. Today's readers marvel at Jesus' miracle-working when he fed the five thousand (Mark 6:35–44). Indeed, he did a miraculous work, and it is appropriate for us to be in awe. But we often miss an intriguing feature in the story. Christ very deliberately employed the labor of his disciples—including our emotionally clumsy, albeit still-developing leader, Peter.

When the disciples presented Jesus with the scenario, he responded: "*You* give them something to eat." He was challenging them to take action and solve the issue. When they responded with the probable impossibility of coming up with that volume of food, he sent them off to ascertain what assets were available. They reported back to Jesus, having found just five loaves and two fish. Unfazed by the small count, Jesus proceeded to instruct them in how to organize the people in groups on the grassy field. He took the small resources in hand, gave thanks toward heaven, and then began dividing the pieces.

> Our emotional framework for working to meet serious needs can be forever changed. We entrust Christ with the resources in-hand, follow his directions, faithfully join him in his work, and confidently watch him supply.

When exactly did the fish and bread morph into more pieces? There is some undeniable mystery about those moments. We cannot know precisely, but it appears that as he placed the loaves and fish in the disciples' hands to distribute, the food marvelously multiplied. In the moments to follow, it became a flourishing feast. The crowd had their fill. The disciples then worked cleanup, picking up twelve baskets of leftovers. For thousands of people, it was the unforgettable picnic of a lifetime. For the disciples, their perspective on how God works—their own emotional framework about working to meet serious needs—was forever changed. The disciple's role was to access assets, entrust Christ with the resources in-hand, follow his directions, faithfully join him in his work, and confidently watch him supply. The pattern was undeniable. Jesus was working to produce the outcome, but he was using his disciples to join his action-oriented mission.

A win-win in the blessing business

Believe it or not, such mission to bless is not just beneficial to the recipients—the poor, the needy, the widows, and the foreigners whom you bless with such loving good news and good works. It's also extremely good for you, the one extending the blessing. An intentionally laser-like focus on God's mission to bless others proves seriously healthy for your own personal emotions. Over time we can discover that God's mission to bless others keeps us motivated, especially when life's circumstances prove so difficult that we want to quit.

Several years ago, a new leadership assignment I (JEP) accepted involved seriously enormous challenges. I was tasked with leading our ministry organization through the potential minefields of risky and essential transition. As often happens, those big changes were met with serious resistance as well as several dozen critics. The heat I took combined with the hits to our organization's overall leadership team proved utterly exasperating.

Outright anger was expressed, and the overall opposition that flew our way came at a level like I had never faced in my previous decade of leadership. Honestly, I was stunned by how people chose to be cruel, even people who claimed to love Jesus. (Okay, I'll admit, I was probably a bit naïve.) During a span of several months, I had people shout at my face, openly mock me, and otherwise vilify my leadership. The season was outrageously painful. Some days, my emotions were just numb with aching, and there were several late nights I slumped into my big chair at home, feeling physical tightness in my chest. At one point, I learned that a group was actually gathering to pray against me as well as the other leaders in our organization. I seriously wondered if we would survive.

During those turbulent months of upheaval, my own leadership was far from perfect. Seriously, God had big lessons to teach me. Multiple times, I needed to seek forgiveness and reframe my perspective as I led our team. With Christ's strength, we persevered through the storm, practiced forgiveness again and again, and trusted God to work his bigger plans.

Two remarkable gifts from God made all the difference. First, we had an amazing team of board leaders. Courageously, they stood by the big vision for essential, mission-advancing change. They prayed hard through the conflict. Instead of running away or caving under pressure, these leaders courageously faced into the conflict and took on difficult conversations with the naysayers. Bold board members worked to protect those of us leading the charge, and they gushed encouragement in pivotal moments. Such loving support from other leaders proved transformative for me and for the entire organization.

And a second gift was transformational for our emotional stability. In that very same season of conflict and change, God was allowing us to live out our mission of blessing others. We began reaching a number of new families, people very new to encountering Christ and embarking on their own faith journey. Icing on the cake, we were blessed with a healthy handful of baptisms across that turbulent year. Hearing those faith stories and watching new people jump in the water kept us focused on the mission Christ had given us. Such life-giving interactions—both the courageous work of board members as well as new people being baptized—served to buoy our spirits and kept us moving forward.

For struggling but emotionally steady leaders, seeing seeds spring up through our mission to bless others reminds us *why* we keep slogging through the tough stuff. Our commission to bless is valuable to our own emotions because it helps us steer clear of navel-gazing and becoming utterly self-absorbed. When I have a seriously crummy week and I'm tempted to cave in, self-implode, or otherwise give in to the dark side, Christ's mission to bless reminds me that I am called to work in such a way that I serve others and bring God glory.

Others-oriented, service-minded vision blesses your own soul. Brownie Wise, that wonder woman of Tupperware, winsomely observed: "When you help someone up a hill, you find yourself closer to the top."[19] Ancient Hebrew wisdom says, "The generous will prosper; those who refresh others will themselves be refreshed" (Prov 11:25). Workplace leaders who lead with resonance discover this win-win. Such laser-like focus on God's mission to bless other people proves seriously healthy, not only for those wonderful people you reach, but for your own emotional development.

No doubt about it, work can feel horribly hard, but it can also become extremely hearty, resulting in very God-honoring productivity. When we choose to view work through God's original design—including his redemptive plans to restore creation—we can adopt a more positive perspective and newfound significance to our daily labors. In addition, we experience stronger, more dynamic teamwork through cultivating resonant, authentic, and caring communication.

Skillful communication is a bold step in smart, well-delivered leadership, and it also helps you grow a vitally healthy workplace culture. A pro-work perspective along with positive communication finds foundational motivation in the Lord's commission for us to bless others—especially those who are needy and previously outside God's family. We can make intentional, creative plans to start new, Christ-honoring businesses, employ needy foreigners, produce amazingly helpful products, and share God's life-changing good news—all with the aim of blessing others and expanding Christ's kingdom work.

Yes, these God-honoring views can fire us up and help our workplaces become seriously adventuresome once again. We might just find ourselves sincerely motivated for Monday—pumped up

---

19. Wise, www.tupperwarebrands.com/company/heritage.

and more positive about going to work. With our next chapter, we'll turn attention toward some even more exciting dynamics that often arrive at the office, storefront, or production floor. What happens when you meet someone attractive? When glances are exchanged and flirtation starts to fly, how do we juggle our romantic emotions in the workplace?

Questions for reflection and discussion

1. What most surprises you in the story of Earl and Brownie?

2. When have you seen emotions play a pivotal role in your daily work, for you personally or for coworkers? What happened?

3. Do you find that most people around you view their work as drudgery, a necessary evil—just a way to eventually enjoy the weekend? Explain. How about your personal view?

4. What stands out as positive about Ruth and Boaz' perspective on work?

5. Would you say you communicate skillfully with your co-workers and contribute to the creation of an overall healthy workplace culture? How do you think others rate your communication skills and your workplace culture?

6. Identify two or three tangible, strategic steps you can take to make your work even more of a mission-focused blessing to others.

7. Describe the difference between the give-a-handout approach and an intentional business strategy that includes dignity-based workspace for those less fortunate?

8. What will it take for you to become a more resonant, emotionally savvy workplace leader?

9. Are there steps you might take, along with other leaders, in order to create new businesses that employ, train, and otherwise bless more people? Would you consider creating such work in another place on the globe? If so, what could get you started?

CHAPTER SIX

Romantic Roller Coasters

He's more myself than I am. Whatever our souls are made of, his and mine are the same.
—EMILY BRONTE IN WUTHERING HEIGHTS

Several years ago, a document began circulating that quickly and creatively grabbed parents' attention. It was simply entitled *Application to Date My Daughter*. Following the typical blanks for name, address, and age, these profound questions appeared on the form:

1. Church? Number of times attended last year?
2. Do you own or drive a van? YES or NO. If YES, discontinue filling out this application.
3. In fifty words or less, explain what the word "NO" means to you.
4. In fifty words or less, explain what the word "LATE" means to you.
5. Where would you least like to be shot?
6. Which is the last bone you want broken?
7. What do you want to be, if you grow up?
8. Please complete this sentence: A woman's place is . . .
9. What is my daughter's name?
10. Whom, besides God, should you fear most?

11. Do you have medical coverage?
12. Do you plan to be buried or cremated?
13. List of references (last three girls you dated; include each parents' name, phone number, and the reason the relationship ended)
14. Please note: If accepted, there will be a fifty-dollar deposit when you pick up my daughter. If you are one minute late in returning, the deposit will be forfeited. If you are more than thirty minutes late, refer to question twelve above.

One of the most emotionally charged arenas of life is romance, especially when you feel you have met the person of your dreams. This is also true for parents and guardians. In Ruth's third chapter, verse one, we read: "One day Ruth's mother-in-law Naomi said to her, 'My daughter, I must find a home for you, where you will be well provided for.'" This was Naomi's way of saying, "In the wake of all we've journeyed through together, you need a good man who will take good care of you. And I've got a plan!" Their journey of grief, the return to Bethlehem, and their experience of seeing God's faithful provision now led Naomi to mobilize toward even more progress and flourishing. Apparently, Ruth's action-bias had a positive, emboldening effect on Naomi, motivating her toward next steps on their journey.

Rollercoasters and emotions

I (JEP) *love* riding roller coasters, and I love the fact that that my boys sincerely enjoy jumping on such thrill rides. This was not always the case. Years back, we were trying to convince our son, Joel, that the biggest coaster at Hershey Park would be a joy to ride. He was very apprehensive. We went ahead and got in the queue, layers deep with people and projected to be over an hour-long wait. As we chatted, his anxiety grew, but we kept coaxing him to stay in line, to just keep considering it. He was not easily convinced, and at one point, he broke down sobbing. We managed to keep him in

Romantic Roller Coasters

line—I'm really not a cruel parent, just intent on proactively building courage. Somehow, we successfully got him on the coaster. He buckled up and enjoyed the ride, actually finishing with a big smile. It was a major transformation from the crocodile tears. (Yes, we have before-and-after pictures to prove it!)[1]

Truth be told, romantic emotions operate a lot like the ups and downs, twists and turns, and the correlating emotions of riding a roller coaster. Consider these feeling-laden, deeply personal questions and issues. *Will I ever find the right person? Might I end up being alone for the rest of my life? Will I ever recover from the loss of that previous treacherous relationship? What about children?—I really want to have kids! I need the financial security of a spouse. I long for the physical closeness and intimacy of a marriage relationship.* These questions and other deep musings can indeed make for a wild ride.

All of these feelings and more were part of Naomi's concern for Ruth as well as the events that unfold as our story continues. With Ruth 3:2, Naomi began to play matchmaker. She explained to Ruth that Boaz, the man "with whose women you have worked," was a close relative. Concerned for their security and the continuance of the family line, perhaps Naomi had the ancient precept in mind from an old covenantal code. God had commanded a method, in case of a husband's death, for another man in the family to serve as husband and carry on the family line. Deuteronomy 25:5-6 instructs:

> If brothers are living together and one of them dies without a son, his widow must not marry outside the family. Her husband's brother shall take her and marry her and fulfill the duty of a brother-in-law to her. The first son she bears shall carry on the name of the dead brother so that his name will not be blotted out from Israel.

What unfolds across the following scenes supplies us with deeper insights into the twists and turns of romantic emotion, including

---

1. View Joel's before-and-after pics at http://johneltonpletcher.com/roller-coaster-before-and-after-pics/.

some important pointers for finding greater confidence and guidance when navigating such roller coaster rides in life.

Desperate housewives' risky plans

Ruth had worked for multiple weeks of the barley and wheat harvests along with Boaz' workers in his fields (Ruth 2:23). While such continued labor probably meant ongoing interaction with Boaz, he was apparently slow to make assertive romantic overtures. (And no, he wasn't the first man—or the last—to be a bit slow in this department.) Naomi explained to Ruth that Boaz would be winnowing barley that very night at the threshing floor. A threshing floor was the communal location where local harvesters tossed sheaves of grain into the breeze. The worthless chaff would be blown away, leaving only the finished grain. On evenings of winnowing, it was also a place for a jubilant meal and celebration.

Naomi instructed Ruth to wash, put on perfume, and change into nice clothes. No doubt about it, this carefully scheming, matchmaking mother-in-law was encouraging Ruth to glam up, to look beautiful and attractive (Ruth 3:3a). The story's earlier work scene in the field, including their lunchtime conversation, revealed sparks of romantic interest between Ruth and Boaz. We couldn't help but sense something flirtatiously productive, more than simply work-related conversation transpiring between them. Now, Naomi's clever plans aimed at advancing flirtation and infatuation toward a more significant relationship. And with a thoughtful reading of the story, we cannot help but note there's even something more provocative in play right here.

Naomi's directions to Ruth include risky business, actions that could easily be interpreted as potentially risqué. Her scheming instructions—go to the threshing floor under the cover of night, stealthily note where he lies down to sleep, then uncover his feet and lie down—are all laced with mystery, intrigue, and sexual tension.[2] "Uncover his feet" can also be translated "uncover

---

2. Linafelt, *Ruth*, 48–49.

his *legs*"—a command that presents suggestive euphemism and sexual innuendo. Naomi's plans push us to wonder, what is this woman really proposing? And even more captivating to our imaginations, what is actually going to happen in the dark with such a rendezvous?

If we wish to always encounter an ultra-sanitized, heroic version of our biblical characters, then we are due for serious disappointments. And should it truly surprise us that Naomi might be suggesting such potentially scandalous actions? After all, as we saw in the opening scene, she and Elimelek had no personal moral qualms over either moving to Moab or marrying their sons off to Moabite women. Recall that both actions were principally taboo according to their faith's moral fabric prescribed in the Torah. Although Naomi had made personal progress on her faith-filled, emotional journey, we cannot conclude that she quickly re-learned and applied every inch of God's moral framework. No doubt, she viewed her own newfound, bold initiative as motivated by a situational ethic—to gain financial stability and continue the family line. Perhaps her strategies were born of necessity, pragmatically essential for responsible family preservation.

Tom Nelson readily observes, "When it comes to sexual temptation in the workplace, we don't have to go out of our way to look for it; it often finds us."[3] Attractive people, potential romantic liaisons, and oh-so-risky scenarios unfold daily in our current-day workplaces. Temptation runs rampant. Place people together for extended blocks of time, working close on endeavors of big consequence, and the affection temperature is bound to rise. Glances are exchanged and soon feelings are shared. Flirtation seems innocent, but sparks begin to fly. Then all too quickly, something hotter kindles. So how can we develop an emotional framework for sexual integrity in our workplaces, a wholesomeness that matches God's heart for business

> When it comes to sexual temptation in the workplace, we don't have to go out of our way to look for it; it often finds us.
>
> —Tom Nelson

---

3. Nelson, *Work Matters*, 173.

leaders and workers in every profession? With the choices made in the next scenes of Ruth's story, we gain deeper insights for navigating and growing via such romantic scenarios.

Cold feet in the steamy darkness

Ruth followed through with Naomi's directives. She headed to the threshing floor, and watched from the shadows as Boaz lay down to sleep at the end of his heap of harvest grain. Creeping near, she uncovered Boaz' feet, and lay down (Ruth 3:6–7). Whatever level of heightened mystery—even sexual intrigue and literary tension the storyteller deliberately created for us, the subsequent narrative sequence and conversation yield healthy evidence that what transpired was a *literal* following of Naomi's words. Boaz' actual legs and feet were uncovered, instead of Ruth acting out some sexual fulfillment of the euphemistic expression. No doubt about it, the scene is ripe with language of sensuality, potential fertility—both in agri-business and human fruitfulness. The moonlit scene is indeed filled with romantic intentions. But Ruth *literally* uncovered his lower legs, and she literally lay down at his feet. Carolyn Custis James concurs, making these personal observations:

> I find it next to impossible to reconcile the Ruth of episodes one and two with a woman who would stoop to something resembling a *Desperate Housewives* plot to entrap an honorable man like Boaz in a moral dilemma that demands marriage . . . We also know that Ruth and Boaz have both exhibited unusual levels of godly character, and we expect no less from either of them here. They are followers of Yahweh. They live under his gaze. Their actions are motivated by *hesed*, and they are willing to make great personal sacrifices to live faithfully for him—*particularly* in how they relate to others.[4]

The events and dialogue of verses eight and nine prove pivotal to the entire story. Boaz was suddenly startled and jolted from his sleep. He twisted about—"and there was a woman lying at his

4. James, *The Gospel of Ruth*, 141 and 147.

Romantic Roller Coasters

feet!" (Ruth 3:8b). Judy Fentress-Williams observes: "It is not clear what startles Boaz in his sleep. His 'shuddering' could very well be a response to his exposure after having been uncovered, or due to a night wind. It is possible he had a disturbing dream." Stunned from his slumber and unable to see in the thick darkness, he asked, "Who are you?" (Ruth 3:9a) The woman's reply overflows with significance. "I am your servant Ruth," she said. "Spread the corner of your garment over me, since you are a guardian-redeemer of our family."

She identified herself by name, a transparent, self-revealing choice under the cloak of darkness. She humbly referred to herself as his servant or "handmaid," in contrast to how she was referenced thus far as either "the Moabite" or "Naomi's daughter-in-law." Fentress-Williams notes, "In so doing, she chooses Boaz and now offers Boaz the opportunity to reciprocate."[5] Her picturesque request that he spread the corner of his garment over her held vivid, accentuated significance. His immediately uncovered feet were illustrative of her emotionally vulnerable and circumstantially uncovered life condition. She and her mother-in-law were still in desperate need. And Ruth's request for such coverage echoed Boaz' own language from the first day they met in the barley field. Her use of the word *garment* or *cloak* is the same word employed by Boaz when he implored repayment and reward from "the LORD, the God of Israel, under whose *wings* you have come to take refuge" (Ruth 2:12). She had been carefully listening to his every word, and now she was speaking his language. She was saying, "Let God use you to fulfill such coverage—be the answer to your own prayers on my behalf!"

At this immediate juncture in the conversation, Ruth went rogue, departing from Naomi's script. Naomi had asserted that Boaz would tell her what to do (Ruth 3:4). Instead, Ruth courageously led the way with a daring proposal of her own. Her request that Boaz spread the corner of his garment to cover her carried the bold, emotional-relational request: "Marry me!" Yes, Ruth was

---

5. Fentress-Williams, *Ruth*, 96.

proposing marriage with her audacious declaration. It was risky and gutsy on her part.

Note the brilliance, sensitivity, understanding, and clarity of dialog that transpired. Their conversation revealed a complexity of interaction, far from some drunken debauchery and base, illicit liaison that some interpreters try to propose for this scene. Also consider the cadence of Boaz' stunned awakening, skillful question, and subsequent solid reasoning. Such sensible and God-focused conversation serves to further substantiate the above-board nature of their interaction. Although no all-out hanky-panky transpired behind the heaps of harvest barley, their verbal expressions revealed heartfelt desires. Boaz indeed got cold feet on the threshing floor, yes, but the scene's interaction and dialog certainly did heat up between the two. Soulful, romantic intentions were uncovered under the gentle breeze and midnight's moonlight.

Manly terms of endearment

Boaz was seriously moved by Ruth's proposal and made his own verbal moves, reciprocating with words of blessing. (It seems Boaz can't help it. He readily reflects the image of God, just breathing out blessing in all he says and does.) With deep feeling, he affirmed Ruth, praising her for demonstrating even more remarkable *hesed*, once again echoing her God-like loyal love and covenant kindness. He recognized that she had not run after the younger men, either rich or poor in socio-economic status. Though we do not honestly know full details of his age or previous marital status—perhaps he was a widower or perhaps like other patriarchs, he had multiple wives—Boaz was obviously more mature in both numerical age and seasoned perspective.

Don't miss how emotionally tuned-in this guy proves to be. "And now, my daughter, don't be afraid. I will do for you all you ask." He read the situation and Ruth's obvious vibes, whether verbal or nonverbal. "Don't be afraid." His words reveal amazingly healthy male intuition, too often atypical of our gender (yes, JEP is weighing in right here). Guys, perhaps we should sit up, take notice, and take some cues from Boaz' impressive sensitivity. He's listening and picking up on what he senses from Ruth. His words border on being angelic in the scene. Across the overarching biblical story, God's mighty messengers' primary proclamation, their most frequent expression is "Do not fear, for I am with you!" Boaz echoed this essential encouragement as he promised to do what she had asked (Ruth 3:11).

Terms of endearment continued. His words of warmth affirmed Ruth as a woman of "noble character" or "genuine excellence." Intriguingly, Boaz' assessment and character description of Ruth matches the precise language our story's narrator used of Boaz himself in chapter two, verse one. He was a man of exceptional character. She was a woman of exceptional character. Together, it would appear they are the perfect match for each other.

For several years, I (JEP) worked in a college environment alongside a single guy who got teased by others for not yet being married. Tim was and is an amazing man, full of creativity, serious love for God, sincere love for others, and he carried a Boaz-like reputation. The halls of our institution were filled with seemingly eligible females, many who might have fit the bill as eligible bachelorettes for my friend. While he dated just a few gals across a decade, no one seemed to be his Mrs. Right. Over the years, Tim was verbally hassled by many people who told him that he held way too high a set of criteria for a future wife. Whenever he heard such, he would just chuckle and say, "Well, my Dad's always passed along this wisdom. 'When it comes to finding a life mate, don't settle at finding someone to spend the rest of your life with; find the one you can't live without!'" So Tim waited, and actively watched, and waited some more.

One day, when he least expected meeting someone, along came Sarah. They had only been dating several weeks, and Tim knew she was the one. "I've fallen for her, Pletch," Tim told me with a big grin. "Seems like we're the match. I'm thinking she's a keeper!" They married, had three amazing kiddos, and they have been faithfully serving Christ and others for over twenty years together. Still today, when asked about his uber criteria and his long holdout across those years, Tim smiles and says, "When it comes to love and marriage, I'm so glad I followed Dad's advice. It pays to wait for someone you can't live without. Sarah is proof!"

Some rascally red tape in redemption

Naomi and Ruth were appealing to the ancient code, often referred to as the *levirate* law, that called for a close relative to marry a brother's widow, have a son, and thus maintain the family line (Deut 25:5–10). But with Ruth's proposal, she referred to Boaz as a family redeemer, a role with even more significance than Naomi's original reference to him as simply a close relative (Ruth 3:2). Uniquely, Ruth now called him a kinsman-redeemer (Ruth 3:9). If he assumed this role, Boaz would also hold the responsibility to buy back Naomi's land, in light of her impoverished condition (Lev 25:23ff). Though Ruth may have held little if any grasp of the full legal ramifications between a potential marriage and the man's correlating responsibility to then redeem Naomi's portion of family land, Boaz was fully aware. Based on his response, she quickly discovered the potential snag.

By this point in Israelite history, the two responsibilities, both marriage and land redemption, had become intertwined. Boaz explained that there was another man who was actually a closer relative and therefore someone with first eligibility to fulfill this role. "Stay here for the night," Boaz instructed, "and in the morning if he wants to do his duty as your guardian-redeemer, good; let him redeem you. But if he is not willing, as surely as the Lord lives I will do it. Lie here until morning" (Ruth 3:13). Ruth lay at his feet until daybreak. Concerned for propriety, they made certain that she departed before anyone might recognize that a woman had been at the threshing floor. As she left, Boaz blessed her with more barley.

Arriving back with Naomi, Ruth reported the details as well as his extra-gracious, tangible kindness to provide more grain for food. Naomi soaked up all Ruth shared, and she responded: "Wait, my daughter, until you find out what happens. For the man will not rest until the matter is settled today" (Ruth 3:18).

Romantic Roller Coasters
Enjoying love stories again

You've experienced a full mix of crazy emotions while reading this chapter. Joy and surprise over a budding romance. How about puzzling intrigue over the mildly mysterious, romantic rendezvous? And you've likely felt some awkwardness over how many times we've mentioned sex and sexuality. Some of you are still wondering, *do we really know for certain what exactly went down in the shadows that night at the threshing floor?* (Ah, welcome to the wonder of a good story.)

Some of us grew up in homes where human sexuality was a taboo topic. And it seems these days that every person's family has experienced the devastation of divorce in some proximity to their tribe. As a result, conversations regarding both marriage and human sexuality can carry very raw emotions. Some people stuff their romantic emotions, burying their feelings about sex and marriage. Perhaps you've chosen to become stoic and puritanical in your views and approaches, leaving little room for deeper learning or healthier dialogue, and certainly not anything resembling even a bit of enjoyment related to romance. Other people just throw all caution and self-control to the wind, choosing instead to do whatever feels good in the moment—in the spirit of the judges' days, "whatever seems right in their own eyes."

What if instead of adopting either one of these approaches in our feelings about romance, we would dare to explore God's perspective on our sexuality and the sacred nature of marriage between a man and a woman—through the lens of the biblical story? It's time we learned to enjoy love stories once again. After all, sex and marriage were God's ideas in the first place. What if we began to reframe our feelings about love, romance, marriage, and sex based on God's perspective as revealed progressively across the pages of sacred writ, from Genesis to Revelation?

> What's the big deal when it comes to sexual lust in our workplaces? Our core emotional struggle with lust is that we crave and imagine how people can be *used* for our self-serving interests instead of *genuinely loved*.

What might happen if we mustered some courage to talk with our kids and grandkids about their romantic futures? And what if we were crazy enough to include stories like Ruth and Boaz in the conversations? I can imagine that they might learn how to more graciously respect and responsibly relate to the opposite sex in their high schools, universities, and future workplaces. I wonder if women might discover how to be more assertive. And what if men became better listeners, actually more clued into women's feelings, and skilled in expressing genuine affirmations and romantic feelings?

I have a hunch that engaging conversations around such stories might actually help produce young adults who aren't so scared to get married. They might actually gain fresh faith and hutzpah to do something crazy, daring, and gutsy, like make a lifetime commitment to someone before the age of thirty. (Perhaps they would ground their commitment in *hesed*-style covenant love, that everlasting, won't-ever-quit, Christ-like kind of love.) With conversation around such rich and colorful stories, they might just get the good and holy impression that God is pro-marriage and pro-sex.

Lust, lovemaking, and your soul at work

Diet Coke, circa mid-90s, flaunted one very steamy TV ad. It's comical to review the commercial now. An office full of women suddenly began whispering to each other, "It's 11:30." As the commercial commences, they scurry to the office windows to ogle. A male construction worker on ground level removes his sweat-soaked shirt and begins lusciously drinking a Diet Coke. Apparently, this has become a daily workplace ritual for these women. Though lusting should never be a laughing matter, the commercial's format draws a chuckle twenty years later. The gawking women wear big-framed 80s eyewear and oh-so-poofy hair. The bare-chested, eye candy construction worker is sporting a far-from-chiseled four-pack. And in retrospect, what real man sips Diet Coke anyway?

Romantic Roller Coasters

What's the big deal when it comes to sexual lust in our workplaces? Our core emotional struggle with lust is that we crave and imagine how people can be *used* for our self-serving interests instead of *genuinely loved*. Andy Stanley challenges us on the raw realities of our internal compulsions:

> When left to our private, unaccountable, godless selves, women are still commodities. But let's be honest. This seedy side of maleness is not isolated to computers and clubs. It's everywhere . . . Multiple times a day we are encouraged to think about women as commodities: take them, use them, do whatever we want with them, and then trade them for something of equal or greater value. Worse, from my perspective, is that women are usually the messengers: "Take me, use me, do anything you want with me, and then discard me or trade me in for another one." . . . Males still think like cavemen. Women are complicit. This complicit behavior ultimately undermines a man's ability to have a successful relationship with a woman. Women find that disheartening and at times disgusting.[6]

We shamelessly drool over others, whether in person or in the virtual world, as objects to be randomly consumed, used for our own pleasure and emotional fulfillment.

In our fallen condition and self-centered emotions at work, we drift from God's higher and holier outlook. Frequently, we cave into our own impulses, treating others like commodities. That's why we must regularly reframe our perspectives, working with God's process for the renewing of our minds (Rom 12:1-2). God's style of selfless love aims at practically caring for others' best interests, not using or abusing them.

How do we develop a strategy, to stand strong against workplace temptation? In *Taking Your Soul to Work*, R. Paul Stevens and Alvin Ung share these five strategy steps:

- Know that your heart's desires are for God. Hunger and passion for God put all lesser desires into perspective.

---

6. Stanley, *The New Rules for Love, Sex & Dating*, 104-105.

- Reduce exposure to erotic stimulation in your choice of movies, novels, and Internet sites. Put a plan in place that will help you avoid temptation on business trips.

- Pray for a colleague, a customer, or a supervisor whom you find attractive. Choose God's perspective on the person instead of treating her/him as "just a body" to be visually consumed.

- Seek accountability partners.

- Identify the early beginnings of lustful thoughts. Heightened vigilance in advance allows you to be more responsive to the Spirit's guidance.[7]

Instead of being trapped in daily rituals of workplace lust and other sexual sins, we *can* stand strong. We can run away, stay pure, and truly honor Christ. We can honor others with more wholesome love at work.

When compared to the widespread cultural perspectives of the first century A.D., Christ and Christianity marvelously elevated women's role and status. Christ longed for people to know that women are deeply loved by God. He modeled this perspective in his earthly ministry, and he intends for such pure and wholesome love to permeate our attitudes and actions at work and home. To a male-dominant, first century culture that largely thrived on a base, sensual, "possess and use" view of women, the Apostle Peter encouraged: "Husbands, in the same way be considerate as you live with your wives, and treat them with respect . . ." (1 Pet 3:7). Recall the early version of the developing disciple from whom these sacred words are coming. He was brash, boisterous, pragmatic Peter. He was the impulsive, take-Jesus-to-task, swing-a-sword and slice-off-an-ear, knee-jerk, live-in-the-moment Peter. Now years later, as a seasoned leader, he is encouraging husbands to be considerate and respectful. Can you sense a bit more than just a shade of emotional development on Peter's part? Following Peter's injunction—mirroring Boaz and Ruth's interaction at the threshing

---

7. Stevens and Ung, *Taking Your Soul to Work*, 26–31.

floor—our own current-day conversations can be marked by the highest respect and the noblest of intentions. And such loving, selfless consideration can transpire even while entertaining the joyous thrill of God's intentions for romance between a man and a woman.

Wait

It's a profound and powerful word. Naomi shared it with Ruth as they anticipated Boaz' next-day action with the other potential kinsman-redeemer (Ruth 3:18). Wait. The ability to exhibit such self-control is a rare commodity, a deliberate choice that starts deep in our emotional framework. Will we slow down, thoughtfully deliberate both facts and feelings, and then choose to be calm and controlled instead of quickly caving in, following our impulses, and compromising our character? Carolyn James observes these emotional tensions in Ruth's story, the deep internal struggles the characters faced:

> The narrator has deliberately created a scene riddled with sexual tension, *not* to spice up the story for the sake of sensationalism, but to drive home an important point—namely, that Yahweh's people are perpetually confronted with difficult situations and hard choices. Will they be guided by self-interest or will *hesed* cause them to set aside self-interest and freely sacrifice for others? In every episode of the book of Ruth, one or more of the central characters face that kind of decision, and we repeatedly observe them going above and beyond what duty, custom, and the law require. These are gospel moments—glimpses of the kind of world God envisioned at creation and that Jesus came to restore.[8]

Choosing transformed emotions, the image of Christ, his style of loyal, selfless love will powerfully reframe your inner world, empowering you for skillful waiting.

---

8. James, *The Gospel of Ruth*, 147–148.

EmotiConversations

Urging us to wait patiently and actively follow God's ways on the romantic roller coaster, John Mark Comer references Psalm 37 and David's call for committed patience. Comer encourages us:

> David says, "Just wait. Life isn't over yet." But waiting is hard to do. That's why David's call is to "wait patiently" for the Lord. Not for a man or a woman. Not for a proposal or a "yes." Not for a ring wrapped around your finger, but for God. And don't forget that God is with you . . . He's there. You see, we're not just waiting *for* God. We're waiting *with* God. Waiting is active, not passive. Notice the language. *Trust, do good, dwell, enjoy, take delight in, commit, be still*—seven staccato commands all leading up to "wait patiently" for the Lord. Each one is dripping with implications.[9]

Waiting does not mean you quit and get off the roller coaster—give up pursuing, stop taking risks, only play it safe, or just pray about love. Instead, patiently waiting means you keep rolling forward in bold, obedient action with calm confidence. You let God's presence and loyal, faithful love guide you on the wild ride.

> Instead of being trapped in daily rituals of workplace lust and other sexual sins, we *can* stand strong. We can run away, stay pure, and truly honor Christ. We can honor others with more wholesome love at work.

It's seriously fantastic to realize that God's gracious formation process includes this often-puzzling arena of romantic emotions. And even this important zone of life holds potential for personal growth into the image of Christ, for the sake of others. Along the way, we discover that we are learning to let go of our toxic feelings, to trade what tasted very bitter for God's good plans. Let's take next steps in our story. Is it truly possible to move from sour, ugly tastes to something sweeter and profoundly better?

---

9. Comer, *Loveology*, 160–64.

Romantic Roller Coasters

Questions for reflection and discussion

1. Have you ever seen matchmaking efforts succeed? 'Ever seen them backfire?

2. If you are a parent or grandparent, can you relate to Naomi's concerns and attempts to play matchmaker for Ruth? Explain your feelings related to your own family and romance.

3. Describe some of the romantic rollercoasters you have personally faced. What were your most pressing questions and feelings while riding through that season?

4. What do you find most shocking, risky, or even risqué about how Naomi and Ruth handle the situation with Boaz?

5. How does Boaz' emotional sensitivity impress you? What would it take for you to be a better listener, more responsive to another person's cues, both verbal and nonverbal?

6. How does Ruth and Boaz' conversation reflect the priority and importance of personal character when seeking someone for a lifetime commitment? What does such cultivation of character truly involve?

7. What do you think about this deeper explanation of our problem with lust, the core problem of viewing others as objects to be selfishly consumed? What do you believe could be your best strategies for overcoming sexual temptation in the workplace? How can you implement those approaches?

8. How are you stirred, challenged, and encouraged by Peter's injunction in 1 Peter 3:7?

9. Why do we find it so difficult to wait patiently on God? How can such waiting be transformative to our spiritual-emotional framework?

CHAPTER SEVEN

Bitter to Better—Really?

Each heart knows its own bitterness, and no one else can share its joy.
—PROVERBS 14:10

Green naugahyde, pure pleather, graced the tops of our silver-based swivel seats. As an eight-year-old, my (JEP) feet dangled under the countertop ledge. It was a Saturday morning, and Grandma Hall was grocery shopping at Kroger. Grandpa and I were doing our part, waiting three doors down and carrying on conversation with his cronies at the Sears and Roebuck's front-of-store café. Thick coffee in a quintessential, brown-clay mug was Grandpa's beverage, the perfect accompaniment for fishing and baseball tales with his buddies. My drink order was a Coca-Cola, to be pumped from the machine behind the counter and served in a tall foam cup. The big boys were already deep into a big fish story when mine arrived. With no reason for any hesitation, I took a hearty swig. Instantaneously, it shot right back, out my nose, out my mouth—it felt like out my ears and out my toes.

With slow-motion quality to my current recollection, I still feel it. The supposed Coke had touched my tongue, sloshed into my mouth, and immediately burned with a pungency of flavor and accompanying scent I had never yet experienced. Instantaneously, I rejected it. What I anticipated to be sweet cola was instead a disgustingly bitter liquid. You've guessed it. I was mistakenly served the carbonated, fizzy water with just a remaining hint of drizzled caramel color. The actual sweet syrup normally pumped into the machine's mix had run out. Grandpa's friends got a good chuckle as they helped mop up the messed up countertop, while the café waitress switched the syrup tank and got me a refill. For some reason, to this day when I drink soda pop, I typically take a cautious test sip instead of a whole-hog swig.

What's the normal reaction in your life? We often drink from a bitter cup of life circumstances. What happens deep in your soul? You receive the two o'clock in the morning call, telling you of the shocking death of your coworker. Or there's a major dip in your business' financial bottom line for the third straight month, causing you to lose even further ground. Perhaps your sibling receives diagnosis of a terminal illness. Or your husband loses his job in a sudden, unfair turn of events. What about the egocentric boss who's been driving you crazy for several years, but for some reason during the current season, he's pushing all your buttons and adding gargantuan stress? When you never saw it coming, a family member's addictive, self-destructive habits turned deadly. Or what happens when your best friend's child dies in an entirely nonsensical driveway accident?

How do you or someone you know survive? And how do you do more than just survive? Is there any way to recover, grow strong again, and actually go on to thrive? Might it be possible to emerge on the other side and taste something that is better, sweeter, and more beautiful?

Revisiting bitter cups in Bethlehem

Across previous chapters, we have encountered the rough and tumble of a fractured family in the Old Testament story of Ruth. Some of the darkest days of Israel's history, these were the "days of the judges" when everyone did whatever seemed right in his or her own eyes. In the face of the famine in Bethlehem (aka, literally, the *House of Bread*), Naomi and Elimelek fled to the nearby country of Moab. While residing in this foreign land, Elimelek died and Naomi subsequently lost her two grown sons. After living in Moab ten years, she and Ruth returned to Bethlehem, landing back in the family's original homeland. Finally, food and harvest had returned to the famine-stricken region. Marvelously, the *House of Bread* had bread on the table once again.

Two grieving women, impoverished and struggling, made the trek back to Judah, and they were still wondering how they would survive. Naomi captured the repulsive flavor—her own repulsive mix of frustrations and heartache in Ruth 1:19–21:

> When they arrived in Bethlehem, the whole town was stirred because of them, and the women exclaimed, "Can this be Naomi?" "Don't call me Naomi," she told them. "Call me Mara, because the Almighty has made my life very bitter. I went away full, but the Lord has brought me back empty. Why call me Naomi? The Lord has afflicted me; the Almighty has brought misfortune upon me."

Her self-revelatory new name, *Mara*, means "bitter." Here is an honest, dismal, and desperate declaration, raw and authentic emotions. The "sweet" one is now "bitter."

Motivated by her gutsy, loyal, loving vow (Ruth 1:16), Ruth followed the Hebrew social system's opportunity for the poor to gather leftovers in the fields during harvest times. And she happened to come into the field of an amazing man of influence. Boaz, a man of character and renown, of great devotion to the Lord, was also related to Naomi's family line. This meant he was eligible to serve as a redeemer, a purchaser of family property and guardian for potential family progeny, as prescribed in the Levitical and Deuteronomic codes. Could it be? Might this man help the shriveling family tree to flourish once again?

Last chapter, we faced the edge-of-our-seats question as Ruth approached the threshing floor to encounter Boaz in the dark of night. *Would he be willing to step into the role and marry her?* Previously, romance appeared to spring up between them while conversing over the harvest, including their lunchtime interaction (Ruth 2). In the story's third chapter, Ruth asked Boaz to provide coverage for her and Naomi. If he would marry Ruth and redeem the property, they could potentially keep the family line alive. Such a move on Boaz' part would mean stability, blessing, renewal, and

Bitter to Better—Really?

fresh flourishing again for this family. Could they potentially move beyond being bitter and actually experience life that was seriously better once again?

The family who loses a son at war hears all the platitudes and nice words of gratitude for such ultimate sacrifice. But that mom and dad still wonder if they will ever truly survive emotionally and go on to recover, renew, and thrive again.

> If you've made a bunch of bad business blunders, you wonder. Is there any chance I could pick up the pieces, walk away stronger, and actually find my way back again?

If a relationship near and dear has come unraveled, or you've faced an ugly divorce, or a once-solid friendship has blown apart, you wonder. Can I make any sense of this, really? Will I recover? Can I truly move forward to survive emotionally, to renew, and flourish?

If you've made a bunch of bad business blunders, you wonder. Can we possibly come back? If this big endeavor totally tanks, how am I going to handle it personally? Is there any chance I could pick up the pieces, walk away stronger, and actually find my way back again?

With just a couple bad choices or momentary lapses in judgment, you slipped up, stumbled, and messed up morally. Now you're living with ugly consequences, harsh realities of your sin, and it's utterly painful, oh so bitter. You still wonder, can anything good and beautiful emerge from the ashes? Or has my story gone up in flames with finality?

No doubt about it, life's harsh and tragic experiences can leave us very bitter, angry, peeved, sour, and utterly exasperated. Jesus had similar deep emotions in mind when he asked his disciples, James and John, if they were actually able to drink from the cup of suffering (Mark 10:38–39). Christ himself cried out, "My God, my God! Why have you forsaken me?" In bitter anguish, he went on to drink the brew of torturous nails, mockery, and excruciating death on the cross. With our own bitter cups, we wonder, "Why, God?" Can we make any sense of all this? Will anything good come from it? How do we actually move beyond bitter, to get substantially better emotionally?

Legal matters

Ruth—bold and beautiful, loyal and loving—was glowing with growing character. Taking big risks, she proposed to Boaz at the threshing floor in the middle of the night. He gave enthusiastic indication of whole-hearted desire to marry her, but he informed her that there was another man ahead of him, more eligible in the family to redeem Naomi's property and marry Ruth. Boaz promised to talk with him, to determine if he was willing to step up as the family redeemer.

With the opening scene of chapter 4, Boaz conversed with the other eligible redeemer at the town gate. This individual was not named in the story—a deliberate literary device, aiming to downplay this other character's importance and spotlight Boaz' noble choice.[1] Ten additional elders sat down as witnesses, and in no time, there was also a gaggle of townspeople (Ruth 4:9–11). The Bethlehem community circled around to witness what might transpire, a scene rather typical for Judean legal culture. The gate's vicinity served as a Hebrew court, like a council chamber or a clerk's office for transaction of affairs. And the community could opt to listen, watch, and weigh in if they would like. On this particular day and case, the growing crowd was extra-intrigued by what legal issues might be transacted by this renowned, influential businessman on behalf of the two widows. And what might be Boaz' intentions regarding the younger one, the marriage-eligible Moabite?

Though the mystery man was initially willing to redeem the property, upon deeper discussion and disclosure of the details, he explained to Boaz that marriage to Ruth would potentially jeopardize his own estate. So, he was not willing to serve as redeemer. He urged Boaz to enact the redemption. The deal was sealed with

---

1. Sakenfeld, *Ruth*, 68-69.

Bitter to Better—Really?

a unique ceremony, as the next-of-kin removed his sandal and handed it to Boaz (Ruth 4:7–8).

During this era, a person's foot and accompanying sandal could symbolize power and possession, even all-out territorial claims over the land on which one's feet walked.[2] While the explanation of this scene's sandal transaction held some common language with the levirate law of Deuteronomy 25, the outcome of each was distinctly different. The ceremony of Deuteronomy 25 would bestow shame on a brother who was unwilling to marry a widow and continue the family line. By the time we reach the legalese of Naomi and Boaz' day, practices had apparently morphed to include this transaction of the sandal, now denoting a *positive transfer of property*.[3]

Playing big, bold previews

When our family goes to the movies, we make certain we arrive early to get good seats, grouped all together. Once seated, we typically haggle over who is going back out to get popcorn and drinks (or we work to discover who possibly snuck in some kind of candy or goldfish snacks). Finally, the lights dim one level, and the previews begin to roll. As they do, we often execute some form of running commentary and thumbs-up or thumbs-down evaluation regarding how we think each new release will do. Sometimes we groan, thumbs down, and give the flick's preview a gong. We shake our heads. "Looks stupid." Or, "Chick flick alert!"—exclaimed often by my (JEP) all-guy offspring. At other times, when a preview looks sensational and sure to captivate, someone leans forward and says to everyone, "That looks amazing—a must-see!"

With the next conversations at the Bethlehem gate, big previews were played, future projections of what those elders and townspeople anticipated would happen with Boaz and Ruth. What's coming to the screen next? Boaz proceeded to review each detail of

---

2. Hamlin, *Surely There Is A Future*, 58.
3. Fentress-Williams, *Ruth*, 113–14.

the legal transaction with those present, and he reaffirmed that they were all witnesses (Ruth 4:9–10). Then, as the elders and townspeople reciprocated with affirmation, they *played the previews*, voicing immense proclamation of blessing for future thriving.

Seriously stunning are the words we hear when we slow down and sincerely consider what's said in advance of Boaz and Ruth's marriage. The community's verbal expressions were colorfully bold and positively prophetic, presenting enormously long-range implications.

> We are witnesses. May the Lord make the woman who is coming into your home like Rachel and Leah, who together built up the family of Israel. May you have standing in Ephrathah and be famous in Bethlehem. Through the offspring the Lord gives you by this young woman, may your family be like that of Perez, whom Tamar bore to Judah (Ruth 4:11–12).

They longed for Ruth to become like the famous matriarchs of Israel, Rachel and Leah, who were so fruitful for the Hebrew family. These words of blessing also called for Boaz to experience long-term legacy among God's people.

Notice how the community also vocalized a blessing over a potential child, using language that was ripe with promise-fulfilling implications. This is an extra-gutsy preview, when we recall that Ruth and her previous husband, Mahlon, had apparently struggled with fertility issues. A potential child for Boaz and Ruth was literally called *the seed* by these witnesses, a long echo of terminology that started back in ancient biblical scenes. There was the creation seed in Genesis 1 and also the woman's promised seed, destined to be victorious over the serpent (Gen 3:15). Vital to note, the elders and townspeople of Bethlehem fully recognized God's

---

Too often, we play only pervasively discouraging previews of what we assume will be our inevitable fate—forever. We push away from others and so miss the chance to hear life-giving words of hope and future-oriented momentum. If we do draw closer to others, we can open our souls so they can play better previews for us.

role in all that was unfolding. Such *seed* would be given by God and lead to long-range flourishing, similar to Perez' importance in Judah's family line, upon being born to Tamar (Gen 38; Ruth 4:12).

Who helps you play the movie?

When forced to gulp down a super-sized cup of bitter circumstances, how do you normally react in subsequent days and months? Some of us assume a significant level of smoldering victimization. We say things like: "I've been treacherously treated. Now I'm a mess and always will be." Or we collectively spout off, "Life has dealt us a cruel blow, and we feel certain we will never be the same again—most certainly, we can't grow better and move on to thrive."

Quite frequently in the face of bitter times, we say, "Hope? Ha! What a crock! Grow stronger? Me, get better? No way!" We grow cynical, inward-focused, and even self-absorbed. Way too often, we listen to our dismal inner voices, and we play only pervasively discouraging previews of what we assume will be our inevitable fate—forever. We push away from others and so miss the chance to hear life-giving words of hope and future-oriented momentum.

What if we intentionally draw close to others, so we can share from the depths what we are facing emotionally? If we do draw closer to others, we can open our souls so they can play better previews for us. For those of us whose bitterness, victimization, and cynicism land us in the depths of despair, discouragement, and even depression, we need the extra-positive influence of community. Douglas Bloch urges us to intentionally gain a support team. For starters, this team should include a recovery partner and a mental health professional—then move forward to include additional family and friends with whom we can walk.[4] The aim is to gain a community of people who can both hear us out and speak words of blessing, greater hope, as well as fresh, imaginative previews of a preferred future.

---

4. Bloch, *Healing from Depression*, 155–56.

EmotiConversations

A big part of our success with such a support team is predicated on growing in vulnerability together. Brené Brown explains: "Vulnerability is about sharing our feelings and our experiences with people who have earned the right to hear them. Being vulnerable and open is mutual and an integral part of the trust-building process." Such genuine openness requires deliberate time invested together, healthy boundaries, and thoughtfully sharing our stories. Brown encourages, "The result of this mutually respectful vulnerability is increased connection, trust, and engagement."[5]

Life-change guru Henry Cloud urges people who are seriously passionate about succeeding in life and love to "play the movie." Cloud describes it like this:

> Successful people evaluate almost everything they do in this way. They see every behavior as a link in a larger chain, a step in a direction that has a destination. And they see this link in both possible directions, the good *and* the bad. They think this way to attain the good things that they want in life, and they think this way to avoid the bad things that they do not want. In short, they rarely do anything without thinking of its ultimate consequence. They play the movie . . . Any one thing you do is only a scene in a larger movie. To understand that action, you have to play it out all the way to the end of the movie.[6]

Henry proposes that we think very intentionally in advance about the longer-range, macro-view of the potential outcome with any given situation, and then carefully make our choices coincide with our desired outcomes.

Such life skill holds humongous implications for your future career path, stronger business networks, romantic connections, financial investments, and prioritization of family time. While such choices come deeply wrapped in your own personal, emotional framework, long-range perspective can easily become blurred and foggy based on your own preconceived notions, jaded judgment, and even smoggy, self-centered motives. Here's where having a

---

5. Brown, *Daring Greatly*, 45–46.
6. Cloud, *9 Things You Simply Must Do*, 72.

team of people around you—others who can more objectively play the previews— will immensely contribute to seeing with larger perspective. Such friends and family can help you see longer-range and think about the future implications. And they can help you see better, stronger, healthier pictures, to engage in holy imagination of God's preferred pictures for your life.

A better future, in his hands

If anyone held a legitimate reason to be bitter, it might have been Jimmy Braddock. In a season when everything had been looking up, suddenly, life slid desperately low for Jimmy. His career rapidly declined, and people began viewing him as a washed-up loser. To make matters worse, just as his livelihood and public image were taking a slide, the nation began its descent into the Great Depression. You might say the Stock Market crashed in 1929, and so did Jimmy Braddock.

James Braddock never had life easy. He was born in the Manhattan neighborhood then known as Hell's Kitchen, New York, in 1905. He was the sixth of seven Braddock children. His parents were hardworking, Irish immigrants. Eager to escape the squalor of Hell's Kitchen, Jimmy's father moved the family across the Hudson River to West New York, New Jersey. They were a poor family, but Joe Braddock did scrape up enough money to send his children to a parochial school. However, Jimmy did not like school and was not a good student. He was very good at one thing—fighting. His favorite part of each school day was recess and the inevitable fight in the schoolyard. Jim was tough, and win or lose, he never quit. When Jim Braddock turned fourteen, the nuns at school decided he already had enough education. Jim left school and immediately began finding odd jobs to help out his family.[7]

In the early part of the twentieth century, boxing was the most popular sporting event in America. Baseball was coming into its own, but all middle class and lower income families faithfully

---

7. Schaap, *Cinderella Man*, vi-46.

followed "the fights." People regularly listened to matches on the radio or read blow-by-blow accounts in the newspaper the following day. Jim's brother, Joe, became a boxer, and a few years later he helped launch Jim's career as an amateur prizefighter. From 1924 to 1926, young Jim Braddock was the terror of the Garden State's amateur ranks.[8]

When he was twenty years old, Jim was encouraged to move his career into professional ranks, and he chose the official name of James J. Braddock. His career took off when his management was turned over to Joe Gould. With keen sense, Gould knew what it would take to develop Jim's skills into those of a winner. Jim's record was solid. Along with typical wins and losses, he held twenty-one knockouts as a light heavyweight. His finest strength as a fighter was in his powerful right hand.

Unfortunately, everything suddenly changed when he broke that hand with a punch to an opponent's skull. Injuries to his right hand quickly became chronic and greatly impacted his career. Over the next couple of years, he continued to fight, but his performance was lackluster. He began having trouble getting bouts with decent opponents. Over time, he was being viewed as a has-been fighter with no real future. The final devastating blow hit when the Boxing Commission suspended Jim's professional license to box.

During those years, Jim had married Mae Fox, and they had three children. To accent support for his young family, he had invested some of the winnings from his boxing career in a taxi company. The business did reasonably well until the Stock Market Crash of 1929 ushered in the Great Depression, and soon, the taxi company failed. It was very difficult for Jim to find work, and his family felt the devastating impact of their financial losses.

Jim and Mae were forced to move the family into a very small basement apartment. There was never enough money for necessities like food, clothing, and utilities. Each morning, Jim left home and walked for several miles seeking any form of work he might find. More often than not, he returned home without success. During these days, Jim fell into a period of dark bitterness and

---

8. Ibid., 29.

BITTER TO BETTER—REALLY?

despondency. Finally, he had to accept public assistance in order to survive and keep from splitting up the family. He was humiliated and depressed.

His right broken hand, very slow to heal, was still in a cast. This made it even more difficult for Jim to find manual labor. At long last, he was chosen for a work crew on the docks, loading and unloading heavy cargo. It was a long, cold walk to the docks each day, and Jim had to hide his broken right hand. He used only his left. At first this left hand was weak and awkward. Jim was often frustrated, but he knew he had to tough it out and keep up with the other longshoremen. Jim labored on day after day in spite of his pain and bouts of bitterness and depression. His family desperately needed him, and he kept the hungry faces of his beloved wife and children always uppermost in his thoughts.

Then remarkably, everything changed on June 12, 1934. Joe Gould, Jim's old manager, found him working at the docks. Braddock had not had a fight in nine months. Gould was amazed to find Jim in remarkable shape. Although he appeared a bit lean, his powerful arms now looked like lethal weapons. The daily grind of hard work on the docks had not only kept Jim in shape, but the excruciating labor had actually strengthened him. Not only had his right hand healed at long last, his left was now equally strong and intuitively useful.

Gould had an interesting offer for Braddock. Jim could make a quick two hundred and fifty dollars if he would serve as a fill-in fighter against Corn Griffin. It was a short-notice offer. The fight was just two days away. Jim needed money badly, so he agreed. For the first time in a very long time, he felt a heavy load lift from his spirit, and he could breathe again. This was the most money Jim had seen in a long time. He shrugged off his bitterness and dumped his depression. Jim knew he needed to win, not just fill a spot

> The daily grind of hard work on the docks had not only kept Jim in shape, but the excruciating labor had actually strengthened him. Not only had his right hand healed at long last, his left was now equally strong and intuitively useful.

in the ring. He was fighting for his family. He was determined. He would be back in the game with great gusto.

No one expected Jim Braddock, now nothing more than an afterthought, to win that boxing match. But two days later, he clobbered Griffin for the win. After this triumphant comeback fight, Jim went back into serious training. Gradually, new matches came his way. Very soon, he was winning each bout. To his delight, he began to pull his family out of poverty. He paid off bills and stayed current. With healthy pride, Jim went to the city municipal building and not only had his name removed from the relief rolls, but he also paid back all the government assistance he had previously received.[9]

On June 13, 1935, thirty thousand fight fans crowded into the Madison Square Garden Bowl to watch James J. Braddock challenge Max Baer, the Heavyweight Champion of the World. Millions of others listened breathlessly via radio, cheering for Braddock, in spite of the fact that his odds of winning were slim. He was certainly considered the underdog. The press viewed the fight as a bit of a joke, and some even feared that Baer might kill Braddock. That was exactly what had happened to another opponent who had previously dared go up against the Champ.

The night of the fight, Braddock and Baer both slugged furiously. To everyone's surprise, the underdog and once-washed-up boxer was holding his own against the powerful champ. Astonishingly, as the rounds unfolded, not only was Braddock holding his own, he was wearing down the goliath-like Max Baer, landing strategic and timely blows. That night's World Heavyweight Championship lasted the full fifteen grueling rounds, with both fighters still standing. It would end with the judges' decision. Ring announcer Al Frazin walked to the dangling microphone. The crowd went wild as Frazin made the announcement. James J. Braddock was the new Heavyweight Champion of the World. Immediately, the same newspapermen who had once dubbed Jimmy Braddock a washed-up loser called him "Cinderella Man." Remarkably, Braddock allowed his great adversity to do a work of transformation inside him. Both in body and spirit, he moved from bitter to better.

9. Ibid., 187-225.

Bitter to Better—Really?
Tasting something so much sweeter

Boaz and Ruth married, and just like their movie preview revealed, their union resulted in a son (Ruth 4:13). However, the storyteller shares with great specificity that "the LORD enabled her to conceive." Let's be clear. Boaz and Ruth worked hard during the harvest. They fell in love, made romantic overtures, engaged each other with emotional integrity, and encountered the community's blessing. The couple married and made love. We dare not miss it. Humans were working and doing their part, but ultimately, God was working to make something beautifully better from what had previously tasted so bitter.

Swiftly, the focus returns to our original lead character, Naomi. The women of Bethlehem praised the LORD, recognizing his provision of a kinsman-redeemer (Ruth 4:14). They spoke affirmations of how this child signified renewal and sustenance for her in her old age. And whereas when first arriving in Bethlehem, Ruth was tucked in the shadows behind Naomi and labeled "the Moabite," the women now exclaimed: "For your daughter-in-law, who loves you and who is better to you than seven sons, has given him birth" (Ruth 4:15).

> Humans were working and doing their part, but ultimately, God was working to make something beautifully better from what had previously tasted so bitter.

Recall Naomi's personal tirades, her catharsis in the opening scenes. To her daughters-in-law, she vented: "It is more bitter for me than for you, because the LORD's hand has gone out against me!" (Ruth 1:13). And upon her arrival, to the gathered women of Bethlehem, she complained, " . . . the Almighty has made my life very bitter. I went away full, but the LORD has brought me back empty" (Ruth 1:20-21).

Pause to seriously soak in the present scene. Consider what has remarkably transpired. After all of the desperation, grief, fear, and bitterness, Naomi is now holding a child in her lap and caring for him. In those moments, she heard the women of Bethlehem—probably some of the same women who heard her spout off bitter words that day she returned to Bethlehem—now praising God and proclaiming, "Naomi has a son" (Ruth 4:16-17). John Tornfelt winsomely queries: "Can you picture the change, the utter transformation in Naomi? She has gone from being eaten alive by bitterness to being a caring, adoring grandmother."[10]

There's no doubt about it, Naomi morphed from desperately bitter to delightfully better. But astoundingly, the family story is not yet complete. Better days for Naomi, Ruth, and Boaz are not actually the final culmination. What unfolds next may stun you. Truth be told, the acquisition of better movie scenes in your life and mine are not actually the grand finale you might suppose God is aiming to accomplish. In our wrap-up chapter, we'll glean rich insights regarding God's long-range, redemptive intentions.

Questions for Reflection and Application

1. How well can you relate to something being bitter, harsh, or disgusting to your taste? How do you respond?

2. What were the primary indicators in various conversations, demonstrating that Naomi wrestled with deep discouragement and bitterness? What scenarios have you experienced that cause you to say, "I get it! I know what she was feeling"?

---

10. Tornfelt, *Reunion*, 85.

Bitter to Better—Really?

3. The townspeople spoke life-giving words for Boaz (Ruth 4:8–12). Who helps you see life's bitter experiences with better perspective? Who are the people you can count on to "play the movie previews" for you, to help you see how you can thrive and flourish once again? How can you identify and pull closer to such encouraging, empowering people?

4. Do you have several people with whom you are building trust and developing greater vulnerability? If so, what does vulnerability look like and how has it grown? If not, what steps will you take to cultivate such trusting and transparent relationships?

5. What do you find most inspiring about Jim Braddock's story?

6. Is there a current scenario in your own life where you long to morph from desperately bitter to delightfully better? What new perspectives will you adopt or what steps will you take in order to embrace God's transformative process?

CHAPTER EIGHT

Redemption's Long-Range Reach

I'm prepared to contend that the primary location for spiritual formation is in the workplace.

—EUGENE PETERSON

On a warm summer day in the late 1930s, Janet attended a baseball game with her friend, Izzy. After the game, she coaxed Janet, "Come on, I want to show you something fun and fascinating." They walked across the parking lot and arrived at a Model A Ford. "Jump in!" Izzy encouraged. "Listen to this!" She turned a knob, and music began emanating from the dash. In the 1930s, the car radio was an innovative feature, still a rather expensive accessory. "Whose car is this?" Janet asked. "It's Cheesy Hall's," Izzy replied. "He was playing ball in the game we were watching. I think he might have installed this himself." The teenage girls were mesmerized and enjoyed several minutes of listening to big band tunes. Suddenly, out of nowhere, a stunningly good-looking young man appeared next to the Model A. Abruptly—with no greeting or warning—Cheesy reached into the car and snapped off the music. "That's enough! Out, kids! You're going to wear down my battery." The young ladies began to skedaddle. With a flit of her hair and skirt, Janet retorted, "Well, *so* sorry! What a grouch!"

Some meetings appear happenstance and prove that people's emotions can swing quickly. Janet dubbed the debonair Ford owner "moody and grumpy." Little did she know, it would be just a couple short days before she would meet him again.

The work of stories, family trees, and long-term memories

While Ruth's ancient romantic account follows a beautifully stylized plot, portraying well-developed characters and thought-provoking theological priorities, the narrative seems fraught with an obnoxiously awkward conclusion. For present-day readers, this story ends in a most bizarre way.

> Now these are the generations of Perez: to Perez was born Hezron, and to Hezron was born Ram, and to Ram, Amminadab, and to Amminadab was born Nahshon, and to Nahshon, Salmon, and to Salmon was born Boaz, and to Boaz, Obed, and to Obed was born Jesse, and to Jesse, David.[1]

Lines of names, the inclusion of a genealogy, might leave us asking, *Is this any way to end a love story*? At first glance, we are left scratching our heads. However, as we contemplate this intriguing family tree, we arrive at empowering insights. In reality, such a unique literary feature leads us to consider several concluding, thought-provoking concepts. If we consider them carefully, such insights might even morph into deeply emotional and relational applications at work, leading to even greater personal transformation.

For starters, *emotionally robust memories—creatively retold as stories—work to evoke potentially big impact for successive generations*. It should not surprise us that an emotion-rich story like that of Naomi, Ruth, and Boaz would prove so pivotal in God's grand story. For successive generations, this bold and beautiful account has supplied greater confidence in God's *hesed*-thick plans and missional momentum toward redemption.

As present-day readers, we forget that Naomi and Ruth's account would have been passed down via oral tradition across

1. Ruth 4:18–22 (NASB).

thousands of Hebrew families over several centuries. At the very earliest—as evidenced by the genealogy's final listed name—this particular written account was preserved during or just after King David's rule (ninth century B.C.E.). Other scholars, based on various literary clues, place the story's final compilation as occurring shortly after Israel's exile in far-off lands (sixth to fifth century B.C.E.).[2] No matter which time period is assigned for the compilation of this final Ruth account, we are left with the powerful reminder that oral tradition occurred and would have contributed to the collective, long-term memory of God's people. The genealogy serves as a memory jog that this story has been passed down through successive generations.

Johnston and Olson explain a profound link between memory and emotions:

> Emotions seem to function as a memory filter, selecting, rejecting, and enhancing what will be remembered. Without an accompanying emotion, most of our experiences are not remembered at all. Understanding the relationship between emotion and memory has been essential in understanding how memory itself works, but much is still unknown about the partnership of emotion and memory... Investigation of the role of the emotions in memory is some of the most exciting work being done in memory research today.[3]

While such current research has focused on the individual's long-term memory, we cannot help but envision—with further research in coming years—the potential affirmation of correlating benefits for collective communities, families, tribes, and nations. How might whole people groups experience the benefits of collective, emotion-thick, long-term memories via the sharing of oral tradition?

Our own family has a rich oral tradition that goes back multiple generations. Many of my own (HHP) favorite childhood memories are those times when one of my parents would share a memory

---

2. Fentress-Williams, *Ruth*, 21–23.
3. Johnston and Olson, *The Feeling Brain*, xv.

of their childhood or relate a story about some distant ancestor who died long before I was born. The stories were always painted with vivid colors that included unique characteristics of the person, the story's setting—including details of the house, farm, or town—and a bit about the culture and time period. Not all of the characters were heroes and heroines. Each had their own set of flaws, and some were true rascals.

> Emotionally robust memories—creatively retold as stories—work to evoke potentially big impact for successive generations. Stories supply greater confidence in God's *hesed*-thick plans and missional momentum toward redemption.

At our evening supper table, my brothers and I were encouraged to share the events of our day. Over time, we learned how to develop our own stories, and many of those have also become a part of the family lore. I was so fortunate to marry a man who also knew much about his family, and over the years he began to share as well. We encouraged our children not only to listen and remember these tales, but also to value them and relate them to their own children. These family stories recount good times, bad times, happiness, and great sorrow. Often, the stories correlate with a beloved object passed down from generation to generation. Indulge me for a moment. Consider this one.

A small pair of black wool mittens, they were obviously intended for a young child's tiny hands. The mittens, held together by a knit cord, amaze me. The stitches are so precise. The work looks perfect. My grandmother knit the mittens when she was just twelve years old. Now they are lovingly placed on our family Christmas tree each year. The tradition of using them as a tree decoration goes back as far as I can remember. There are many ornaments on our tree that have stories attached, but the mittens are my favorite.

My grandmother, Lillian, was born in 1885. The oldest of five surviving children, she grew up in Bad Axe, Michigan. Her father was a burly German lumberjack, a good, hardworking man who spoke very little English. Her mother was a frail, petite woman from a proud English family in New York. They could trace their roots to the early Puritan colonists of the Massachusetts Bay Colony.

These were still rugged days for a family living in the "thumb" of the Michigan lumber region, and now Lillian's dear mother was dying of pneumonia. Her grandmother and spinster aunt would eventually come from Buffalo, New York, to help with the children. However, until they arrived, Lillian would shoulder the responsibility for her siblings. And remember, she was just twelve years old. As part of her intentional care, she knit mittens and socks for the children. In those days, knitting was not just a pleasant hobby. It was a necessity. All members of a family must be kept in warm wool socks, hats, and mittens to ward off the frigid Michigan winters.

I have often pondered what thoughts must have been going through my grandmother's young mind as she knit. How much love and sorrow must have filled her heart as she grieved over her mother? To encounter so much grief at such an early age without many others around to help seems almost beyond my imagination.

This profound experience of deep sorrow at such an early age must have provided early preparation for the endurance she would need many years later in facing the death of her toddler son. She and my grandfather served as missionaries in a remote jungle in Africa. One day, their child died quite suddenly in my grandmother's arms. Thousands of miles from home, they had to face the death of their oh-so-loved firstborn without the solace of family or friends. Nevertheless, they faced that dark storm courageously and continued on with their work, wholeheartedly serving the Lord.

I inherited the small black pair of mittens the first Christmas after my own mother went home to be with the Lord. As I placed them on my Christmas tree, the family story that accompanied the mittens came to mind and was strangely comforting to me. That year, I decided that I would learn to knit. I would knit my tears and sorrow away just as Lillian must have done so many years ago. I thought of the many stories told by my mother over the years. My soul is rich with so many fond, loving memories of my parents and of family members that I never had the honor of meeting face to face. It is as if I knew each one of them, in spite of the fact that we never physically met, and I have loved them all.

Do family stories, shared over multiple generations, morph in color and emotional texture across time? Of course they do. However, these slight variations and enhancements do not lessen the value of sharing an oral tradition. Numerous generations of families—like those following long-term in Boaz and Ruth's family tree—have valued oral tradition and kept family history alive by verbally sharing. Some current-day scholars are concerned that with the written word and contemporary media, we may be ignoring the great value of our oral traditions that can be passed down to future generations. While committing these tales to the written and digital page is certainly important, so is the spoken story that embeds in the hearts and minds of our children. Not only can these great stories be quickly recalled by memory in order to comfort, instruct, build character, and even amuse us around the dinner table, they can also give each of us a wonderful sense of love. Deep-rooted confidence and family identity are irreplaceable traits for long-term emotional stability.[4]

The work of serendipitous meetings

A second conclusion flows from the unique wrap-up to Ruth's story. *God actively works in our daily happenstance, even as we faithfully work.* It's stunning to consider—such a family tree might have never emerged if Ruth had not gone to work. This genealogy serves as definitive evidence. Remember, the family line had been in serious jeopardy. In that dark and stormy season, it looked like the promised seed might never even have a chance to sprout. But now, these lines of names reveal that the family had flourished. And consider it—God's big plans unfolded through a daily workplace, a harvest field.

An intriguing comment appears back in Ruth, chapter 2—a statement that we deliberately saved for summative comment in

---

4.. See Grandma Lillian's hand-knit mittens by visiting http://johneltonpletcher.com/grandma-lillians-mittens/.

this moment. When Ruth expressed her eagerness to go glean and Naomi gave her the okay, the account says, "As it turned out, she was working in a field belonging to Boaz, who was from the clan of Elimelek. Just then Boaz arrived from Bethlehem . . ." (Ruth 2:3–4). "As it turned out" is a curious, captivating phrase in the ancient Hebrew language. Literally, it says: *her chance chanced upon.* The Theology of Work Project sheds bright insight for us on this quirky little statement:

> God uses apparently chance events to empower people's work. One of the ways God fulfills his promise of fruitfulness is his mastery of the world's circumstances. The odd construction of "her chance chanced upon" (rendered, "as it happened" by the NRSV) in Ruth 2:3 is deliberate. In colloquial English, we would say, "As her luck would have it." But the statement is ironic. The narrator intentionally uses an expression that forces the reader to sit up and ask how it could be that Ruth "happened" to land in the field of a man who was not only gracious (Ruth 2:2) but also a kinsman (Ruth 2:1). As the story unfolds, we see that Ruth's arrival at Boaz' field was evidence of God's providential hand . . . What a dreary world it would be if we had to go to work every day expecting nothing except what we ourselves have the power to accomplish. We must depend on the work of others, the unexpected opportunity, the burst of creativity, the unforeseen blessing. Surely one of the most comforting blessings of following Christ is his promise that when we go to work, he goes to work alongside us and shoulders the load with us. "Take my yoke upon you . . . for my yoke is easy, and my burden is light" (Matthew 11:29–30). Ruth did not have the words of Jesus, but she lived in faith that under God's wings, she would find all that she needed (Ruth 2:12).[5]

As it turned out proves to be far from a statement of luck, good karma, or the universe smiling on her. Through all your daily circumstances—even seemingly mundane details like where you walk at work—you can see God working.

5. Theology of Work Project, http://www.theologyofwork.org/old-testament/ruth-and-work.

Redemption's Long-Range Reach

Do you live with faith-filled anticipation that God is working in and through your daily endeavors? Bill Peel and Walt Larimore remind us, "When we work to meet legitimate human needs, we are working for God and God is working through us, whether we realize it or not. We have a God-given purpose to steward His creation and contribute to human flourishing."[6] Consider these personal assessment questions:

> God actively works in our daily happenstance, even as we faithfully work. It's stunning to consider—such a family tree might have never emerged if Ruth had not gone to work.

- Do you pray about your daily work, asking God to help you be a serious blessing as you "rule and reign" in your tasks (Gen 1:26–28)?

- While leading teams, designing plans, slogging through details, creating new products, building culture, and ultimately serving Christ and others, do you watch for opportunities to see God at work?

- Do you attitudinally embrace the ministry of the mundane, believing God is working even there—even in chores like doing dishes and changing diapers?

- Are you developing your perception skills, to see God unfolding his plans in your daily tasks, relational connections, and opportunities to share Christ with coworkers, clients, and other business contacts?

Indulge me (JEP) please for a moment of further family storytelling.

The grouchy young man, affectionately dubbed "Cheesy" by his friends, was actually named Everett. As a young kid on the playground, he strutted around with a chunk of cheese in hand. He loved to nibble on cheese, so friends teased him, called him Cheesy, and the name stuck. Now nearly twenty years old, Everett Hall got scolded when he arrived home from the baseball game. Izzy's mother had called his mother and tattled about how rude

---

6. Peel and Larimore, *Workplace Grace*, 37.

Everett had been toward the two teenage girls. She reassured that Izzy could handle it—she had known Everett for years—but Janet was new to town, and certainly would have formed a poor impression of Everett. His mother scolded him and insisted that he plan to apologize to Janet—and that he do so soon.

Two days later, Everett stepped onto her family's front porch, knocked on the wooden door, swallowed hard, and said he was sincerely sorry for being so gruff. "Would you like to get ice cream with me on Friday night?" Everett and Janet went out for ice cream, fell in love, and married two years later. In the years to come, they had two boys, Bob and Buzz, and one little girl named Holly.

It's always curiously fun to conjecture. In this case, I can't help but wonder. What if it hadn't been for three innovative, hardworking young men, William Lear along with Paul and Joseph Galvin? They developed the first automobile dashboard radio and named it the "Motorola"—the radio installed in Model A Fords across the 1930s.[7] I find it stunning to consider that my grandmother and grandfather might have never gotten together had it not been for the invention and production of the car radio.

And there is an even deeper conjecture that stirs. What if my grandfather had not been sensitive and responsive to his mother's critique? What if he had been emotionally unintelligent, refused to swallow his pride, and failed to step up on the porch and apologize? Simply deduced, neither John Elton Pletcher nor Holly Hall-Pletcher would be hanging in branches of the family tree. And you would certainly not be reading our book. Now, there's something to get emotional over.[8]

Our work, in tandem with God's work, can bless and redeem others.

A third conclusion unfolds at the story's wrap-up, holding big potential for personal application. *Our daily business and work*

---

7. Lendino, "The History of the Car Stereo."

8. View vintage pic's of Janet and Cheesy by visiting http://johneltonpletcher.com/vintage-family-pics/.

endeavors can leave a definitive, emotional-spiritual impact toward others' redemption, especially for people who are not yet a part of God's family tree. Don't forget, Ruth was previously an outsider, riffraff from Moab. Don't forget, Boaz and his team took a risk, included her on their labor force, and very deliberately embraced God's mission.

Workplace leaders dare to risk, step outside their comfort zones, and develop holy anticipation for what God might accomplish with each of their relational opportunities. In *Workplace Grace*, Bill Peel and Walt Larimore encourage us:

> Whether we work on a factory floor, in a cramped cubical, or in the corner office, each of us is significant and every gift is important in God's master plan to draw people to him. He has given us the privilege of being part of the world's redemption. Never forget small things—a word of encouragement or a simple act of kindness—can be used by God to accomplish big things.[9]

In whatever daily work we do, when both our actions and words are carried out in the character of Christ, we can reach others with Christ's redemptive love (Col 3:17, 23–24).

Ralph Broetje had a literal dream one night as a teenager. Ralph explains. "The dream was that I would own an apple orchard and use the money we made to help feed kids in India." In 1968, Ralph and his wife, Cheryl, bought a cherry orchard in Benton City, Washington. During the first three years, the orchard was plagued by a deep freeze, excessive rain, and treacherous fruit flies. It appeared the fledgling enterprise was ruined and ready to fold. Providentially, help arrived when the Broetjes received the immense blessing of financial backing from a dream team of friends. As a result, they were able to persevere and see stable progress across the coming decade.

In the late 1970s and early 1980s, the Broetjes purchased hundreds of acres of sagebrush land in the Columbia Basin of Washington State. This was not previous apple orchard territory. It

---

9. Peel and Larimore, *Workplace Grace*, 79.

was risky, but they began to plant apple trees. The trees grew and the orchard began to thrive. In 1984, the Broetje family embarked on a mission trip to Mexico. Their trip proved to be transformative for their business' entire focus. Ralph explains:

> That mission to Mexico made me realize how hard it was for people there to dream about achieving anything, because the opportunities did not exist. I understood that they were coming to the United States for better opportunities for their families. It gave us more insight into what their needs are, and it reminded me of why we had this orchard. It wasn't so we could keep building things for ourselves. It was so we could try and give back to the families we worked with as much as we can.[10]

In the wake of that trip, the Broetjes have not only developed numerous additional full-time jobs, but a large complex of single-family homes and apartments, available to rent at low cost to year-round employees. In addition, the New Horizons Preschool and Vista Hermosa Elementary (K–6) were founded. The Vista Hermosa Foundation supports local initiatives for families and reaches out to partner with underserved communities around the world. Such partnerships exist in over thirty countries, including Mexico, India, Honduras, Colombia, Uganda, Ethiopia, Kenya, Chad, Haiti, Jamaica, Romania, and the United States.

> Our daily business and work endeavors can leave a definitive, emotional-spiritual impact toward others' redemption, especially for people who are not yet a part of God's family tree.

In recent years, the Broetjes' work has continued to thrive and flourish. They have developed additional endeavors, like CASA LLC and Mano a Mano, supplying further focus on housing and community building. These endeavors contribute to educational outreach and on-farm seasonal housing for workers needing temporary shelter. Today, the Broetje Orchard in Washington State stands out as a blessing business, accomplishing God's mission in amazing ways, both locally and globally.

10. Broetje, http://www.firstfruits.com/company-history.html.

Hold on! Can people really change?

Uncle Charlie died, and upon settlement of his estate, he bequeathed his aged, prized parrot to his nephew, Bill. Bill took the parrot home and quickly discovered that the bird sported a sassy attitude and an equally foul vocabulary. Every other word out of the bird's beak was a filthy expletive or derogatory remark. The nephew tried everything to evoke change. He spoke wholesome and affirming words. He scolded and corrected. He praised the parrot on the very rare occasion when his words were kind. Bill even took him to parrot speech therapy. Nothing worked.

Finally one day, in total exasperation, Bill had experienced all the ugly noise he could take, so he shoved the bird in the freezer. For a few minutes, Bill could hear the parrot yelling and kicking inside the freezer. Then suddenly, there was silence. After a few moments of continued quiet, Bill grew deeply concerned that he might have seriously harmed or even finished off his Uncle Charlie's very valuable bird. Cautiously, he opened the freezer door. There sat the parrot, curiously tipping his head and smiling. Bill extended his hand, and the parrot stepped out, ever so politely. Bill was puzzled. The bird finally squawked, "Please pardon my rude behavior and obscene speech. Squawk! I do pledge that from this day forward, I shall only express myself in gracious words with loving attitudes. Squawk." Bill was totally stunned and was about to ask the bird what had evoked his monumental change. Just then, the bird queried, "Squawk! May I ask what the chicken did?"

> Transformation's work in and through human emotions—including this deep premise of being conformed to the image of Christ for the sake of others—is all predicated on the big, bold assumption that people can indeed change.

Our core concept of transformation's work in and through human emotions—including this deep premise of being conformed to the image of Christ for the sake of others—is all predicated on the big, bold assumption that people can indeed change. Is there any further substantive evidence, beyond this collage of old stories and nice-sounding axioms, proving that such a presupposition rings true?

Consider these supportive concepts. Present-day researchers hold out strong hope for personal change related to human emotions. Johnston and Olson explain:

> Emotions compel us to act. Indeed the root of the word *e-motion* expresses this core feature of emotions: They *motivate* us to do something. . . . How are emotions regulated? What are the best ways to control emotions that may not be socially appropriate or even personally acceptable? The study of emotions holds the promise of better strategies to regulate emotions in ways that don't just bottle them up inside. A relatively new field of inquiry, appropriately known as emotion regulation, addresses these questions, and is one of the most active areas of research within affective neuroscience, with great potential for practical application.[11]

Current emotional researchers study and report with the aim of people experiencing healthier emotional growth, positive progress, and better transformation toward maturity. Mainstream emotional studies hold real anticipation, genuine optimism that people can indeed still change.

Drawing conclusions about patients' development toward emotional intelligence in the face of negative encounters like fear and conflict, Daniel Goleman summarizes the progress:

> By the time the patients had but a few sessions left in therapy, the encounters they told about showed they had only half as many negative emotional reactions compared to when they first started therapy, and were twice as likely to get the positive response they deeply desired from the other person. But what did not change at all was the particular sensitivity at the root of these needs. In brain terms, we can speculate, the limbic circuitry would send alarm signals in response to cues of a feared event, but the prefrontal cortex and related zones would have learned a new, more healthy response.

11. Johnston and Olson, *The Feeling Brain*, xv.

In short, emotional lessons—even the most deeply implanted habits of the heart learned in childhood—can be reshaped. Emotional learning is lifelong.[12]

Such positive perspective on emotional progress—reinforcing that people of all ages *can* change—runs in strong tandem with our Christian concept of spiritual formation.

The holy work of redemption

The bumbling, fumbling, oh-so-slow-to-develop disciple, Peter, might actually be the poster child for spiritual-emotional transformation. Consider it. On the night Jesus was arrested, when bystanders pressed Peter in an attempt to implicate him, he denied knowing Christ. Not once, but three times. The rooster crowed, a sound that echoed guilty voices through his soul as he recalled that Christ foretold Peter would deny and disown him. "And he went outside and wept bitterly" (Matt 26:69–75).

What's stunning is to carefully observe a key leader, the main mover and shaker, in the opening scenes of the historical accounts of the early church in the book of Acts. We are told of a man who boldly proclaimed truth to the rulers and elders in Jerusalem after being arrested (Acts 4). When questioned, he stood courageously for the name of Christ, declaring to these leaders, "Salvation is found in no one else, for there is no other name under heaven given to men by which we must be saved" (Acts 4:12). And the next verse says, "When they saw the courage of Peter and John, and realized that they were unschooled, ordinary men, they were astonished and they took note that these men had been with Jesus." These disciples expressed with determination that they would continue to obey God rather than be intimidated by the Jewish leaders. Pause long enough to let it soak into your soul. The main voice, the ringleader in such a courageous stand, is none other than Peter. Only a few months had passed, but his transformation was remarkable.

---

12. Goleman, *Emotional Intelligence*, 214.

EmotiConversations

Peter's story is proof that people can deeply change, but how? What might be our best catalyst? A phrase tucked within the story in Acts 4 lends rich insight. It says, "Then Peter, filled with the Holy Spirit . . ." (Acts 4:8). This is a strategic echo of what has already been emphasized by Acts' author, Luke, across the opening chapters of this historical record. The Holy Spirit had arrived, and he was transformative.

We *can* change. Peter Scazerro challenges us: "Most importantly, remember that the Holy Spirit who lives within you will guide you into all truth and grant you supernatural power from outside yourself."[13] No matter what we are facing and feeling deep inside, we are not alone. We can know the transforming work of Christ's Spirit and experience ever-increasing emotional growth.

David Seamands encourages us to more fully embrace a growing dependency on the Holy Spirit's work for healing from damaged emotions. Our cooperation with the Holy Spirit and our patient engagement in God's process are essential for change. "You must become a partner with God in this reprogramming and renewal process. Such work is a continual process, not a sudden crisis. I don't know of any single Christian experience that will change your self-image overnight. You are to be 'transformed by the renewing of your mind'" (Rom 12:2).[14]

Declaring his work as our come-alongside Comforter, the Apostle Paul highlights the Spirit's transformative power. "The Holy Spirit helps us in our infirmities" (Romans 8:26a). The Greek word for *help* carries the idea of Christ's Spirit wrapping us on either side in a strong hold of supportive care. Seamands summarizes: "Here is one of the great works of the comforting, counseling Paraclete—He is always available to take hold on the other side of our crippling infirmity, our damaged emotion, our painful hangup. He doesn't leave us because we are damaged or imperfect in our performance."[15] Thus, we discover great confidence and

---

13. Scazerro, *The Emotionally Healthy Leader*, 43.
14. Seamands, *Healing for Damaged Emotions*, 74–75.
15. Ibid., 136–137.

encouragement as we cooperate, allowing the Holy Spirit to pray on our behalf, even when we only feel like we can groan (Rom 8:26b–27).

More names on the family tree—and then some—and even more

We hope you never forget J. Robert Mulholland's explanation of our developmental journey, particularly the unique trajectory of the final phrase. Spiritual formation is "a process of being conformed to the image of Christ *for the sake of others*."[16] There's a long-range reach to your redemption story. Though oh-so-poignant and personal, it's never just about your individual feelings of tragedy or triumph. God is unfolding a longer-range plan, and he always has others in view. Robb Palmer and Heather Welesko have labeled this *narrative viewing*. They explain: "This perspective proposes that *while we live life episodically, we only truly understand it narratively*. Therefore, narrative eyes, or eyes that look for the larger storyline, are necessary to make sense of it."[17] Our dynamic development emotionally—through all of life's individual roller coaster rides—really makes the best sense when we choose to see God's bigger redemptive story. And his story is always radically others-oriented, including more and more new people on the ever-expanding family tree.

The unique finale for Ruth's story, such "ancestry.com" conclusion, actually compels readers—both ancient and current—to step into such a perspective, both for the immediate biblical story and our own stories. After all, the amazing King David emerged from the colorful tapestry of events related in Ruth's account. And don't miss it. The family lineup is not just composed of predictable "holy people," like prophets, priests, and kings. For the shocking makeup of this family tree, God included everyday workers,

---

16. Mulholland, *Invitation to a Journey*, 15.
17. Palmer and Welesko. *The Diamond of Adversity*, 101.

all-out risk-takers, their provocative conversations, and even some folks from the wrong side of the tracks, like Ruth the Moabite.

Amazingly enough, when we reach David's name—the final name in the genealogy—it's still not actually the end of the story. In the earliest strokes of the New Testament, this same family tree is shared again, this time with significant growth and new branches (Matt 1:1–17). At the culmination of this genealogy, can you imagine who emerges? Jesus, the promised seed and king arrived (Matt 1:16). But much like King David, this new king's birth is not even the triumphant culmination of the story. The narrative continues to roll even deeper and ever wider. Christ's arrival, and all the blessings he brings aim to redeem still others (Matt 1:21). Because Jesus saves people from their sins, the family tree will gain more and more names.

God works.

As we cooperate with the Holy Spirit who helps us and prays for us (Rom 8:26–27), notice what kind of fruit God's Spirit produces next. Paul says with confidence:

> And we know that in all things God works for the good of those who love him, who have been called according to his purpose. For those God foreknew he also predestined to be conformed to the image of his Son, that he might be the firstborn among many brothers and sisters (Rom 8:28–29).

God works. He is accomplishing his transformative endeavors, so that we are conformed to the image of his Son. As we cooperate, the Holy Spirit of God uses the Holy Word of God to breathe new Spirit into us, to reawaken and reshape his image in us, to do nothing short of redeem us.

"The good" God works to accomplish from our raw "all things" is not typically our circumstantial happiness or feel-better tranquility, but a longer-reaching redemption that makes Jesus more famous and draws others—more sisters and brothers—into his family of redeemed people.

Redemption's Long-Range Reach

When we intentionally work in step with God's holy principles and passions, he takes our emotional struggles—our deepest crises, fears, and suffering—and works something far more beautiful than we could ever imagine. Palmer and Welesko call this the "So That Principle." We can choose to see suffering as "a work-in-progress that has been allowed to exist 'so that' something might be demonstrated or emerge out from, and by means of, the sufferings." They highlight the potential outcome:

> Sometimes we suffer so that God might bring out of our sufferings that which is redemptive. Such creativity on God's part is particularly seen when we suffer, for while most can respect a deity who offers only good things daily, we truly honor the Deity who can turn bad into good and produce incredible outcomes from horrible tragedies. God, then refrains from interfering with pain and stopping it. He would rather allow it to take place and in Romans 8:28 fashion, work meaningful outcomes from the raw materials handed to him.[18]

Especially note the longer-range *so that*—the marvelously missional outcome Paul highlights in verse twenty-nine. Through God's working with our raw materials, Jesus the Son can take first place, center stage under the spotlight, his one-of-a-kind place, "among many brothers and sisters." What's Paul saying? As you are conformed spiritually-emotionally, shaped more and more into the image of Christ, then more and more people join the family tree. "The good" God works to accomplish from our raw "all things" is not typically our circumstantial happiness or feel-better tranquility, but a longer-reaching redemption that makes Jesus more famous and draws others—more sisters and brothers—into his family of redeemed people.

Perhaps God intends to redeem the deep discouragement you have felt resulting from your most recent dark and stormy season. What if his *so that* involves your experiencing Christ's transformative help and strength through the ugly, painful process? Having walked through the storm and learned to trust him more, you can

---

18. Ibid., 139.

be ready and sensitive to share your story of Christ's hope with a coworker experiencing her or his own dark and stormy tragedy down the road.

It might be that the horrific grief you experienced last year will be worked together by God's masterful creativity, redeemed, and recycled, *so that* you are prepared to comfort one of your sales associates next year when he or she journeys through loss. Perhaps you will have the opportunity to courageously share Christ's loving good news with him and others on your team.

Maybe God allowed your devastating financial crash several years back *so that* you can now share with others the stronger principles—Christ-focused trust, even wiser financial planning, generosity, and God-glorifying flourishing—those values you now hold so near and dear. Is there any chance God faithfully worked you through that devastating time and is now slowly rebuilding your financial world *so that* you can someday coach others?

The emoticon that matters most

As we wrap up our conversation, there is one amazing emoticon we dare not miss. It seems only fair to tell you, this one is so unique that you will never find it on your phone or any other digital device. You might say this one is the classic. In fact, it's not overstating the case one iota to say that this one is the original, the genesis of all emoticons. You will probably be surprised to hear how far back it goes—*multiple millennia ago*, people longed to see this one expressed in their direction. Consider an ancient text:

> Then the Lord said to Moses, "Tell Aaron and his sons to bless the people of Israel with this special blessing: 'May the Lord bless you and protect you. May the Lord smile on you and be gracious to you. May the Lord show you his favor and give you his peace.' Whenever Aaron and his sons bless the people of Israel in my name, I myself will bless them."[19]

---

19. Numbers 6:22–27 (NLT).

God supplied these instructions for the priest's gracious blessing, including a request for the LORD's face to shine—his smile to be expressed toward his people as the ultimate emoticon.

This same phraseology from these priestly instructions in Numbers 6 is used in the Psalter, the Hebrew songbook. The psalmist requests God's gracious blessing and shining face to favor God's people.

> Let God grant us grace and bless us; let God make his face shine on us, Selah.

Then Psalm 67:2 declares the purpose and result:

> so that your way becomes known on earth, so that your salvation becomes known among all the nations.[20]

It is truly remarkable to recognize God's laser-focused intentionality for blessing his people. God's marvelous emoticon, his gracious smile, has a *so that*. His shining favor and blessing came upon his people in ancient Israel—and still comes on his people today —*so that* more people in more places might taste his grace, truly know his saving work, and grow stronger in his family tree.

When all is said and done, God's smile is the ultimate emoticon. And so we pray that through all the emotions you experience on your journey, you will sense his smile, encounter his blessing, and let his image in you make a profound impact on others.

Questions for Reflection and Application

1. Did your family share memories as you were growing up? Does your family tell stories now? Rehearse one of your favorites.

---

20. Psalm 67:1–2 (CEB). And note how the remainder of the Psalm gushes the Gospel, advancing the language of God's blessing and worship spreading among all nations.

2. What role might passing down family stories play in the development of long-term memory? How might such remembering serve in your emotional/spiritual development and that of your children and grandchildren?

3. Do you readily anticipate God's working in life's ordinary events and daily tasks (assisting customers, doing yard work, raising children, purchasing products, leading teams, etc.)? Why or why not? What would it take for you to more readily seek to glorify God in everyday endeavors, even mundane ones (1 Cor 10:31)?

4. Read together Matthew 26:69–75 and Acts 4:8–22. Identify and describe the stunning contrast in emotions. Does comparing these stories prove that people *can* change—to experience deep transformation emotionally/spiritually by Christ's Spirit? Why or why not?

5. What do you find most amazing about the wrap-up verses of Ruth's story? How was God working for long-range redemption (Matt 1:5–6, and 16)?

6. How does the long-range reach of God's redemption encourage you to more fully trust God for his greater good, even through your deepest and most emotional places?

7. Review Romans 8:26–29. Try to envision long-range. How can you anticipate God might use a current, emotionally-charged circumstance to conform you into Christ's image for the sake of others?

Afterword & Acknowledgements

Walls crumble and rocks crash in the depths of the cavern. Gandalf flees across a narrow stone bridge as the Balrog roars and spews flames. The beast threatens to overtake the tiny group who make up the Fellowship of the Ring. As Frodo and friends run ahead, Gandalf suddenly turns and courageously faces off with the Balrog. A grimace of determination emanates from Gandalf's wrinkled countenance as the monster thrashes his fiery whip. The courageous sage slams his staff onto the pavement and shouts those oh-so-famous, punctuated words: "You shall not pass!" The scene is one of the most emotionally-charged moments in *The Lord of the Rings* series and supplies a passionate declaration, oft-quipped and quoted in a rich variety of circumstances.

Upon reflection, I (JEP) recall two Gandalf-like characters, each deeply responsible for pivotal turning points, moments that significantly impacted the pages you just read. Over twenty years ago, while working on my master's degree at Baptist Bible Seminary (PA) and taking spring semester Hebrew, I accomplished something remarkable for the first time in my academic career. With ten days remaining in the semester, I miserably failed my final exam. I was emotionally devastated. Across that school year, I had struggled to juggle the demands of my classes, my high-expectations administrative role at the college, plus year one as a new husband. I had managed to slide by in my classwork, but I had never actually *failed* an exam. Now I stood in Dr. Richard Engle's office with tears in my eyes. The no-nonsense instructor had taught Hebrew for many years, so this was not an unfamiliar cavern for him to run through with a student. Based on my mediocre quiz grades and overall humdrum performance, Dr. Engle did not even have to vocalize. I could read it in his eyes and across his wisdom-creased wrinkles. "You shall not pass!"

I related how disappointed I was with my shoddy performance and how desperate I felt. I entreated him. Was there any way that I could possibly pass the course? With marvelous emotional intelligence, the seasoned professor thoughtfully paused, looked deeply into my eyes, and then extended a thread of hope. He informed me of an end-of-term project, still yet to be submitted. *If* —and he reminded me that he was speaking with utmost contingency—*if* I poured myself into that project with thorough attention and delivered truly rich insights, there was still a chance that I might pass.

Over the next ten days, I squeezed every available moment into research and synthesis of key discoveries. I was determined. The assigned biblical section to receive morphological and philological attention was the narrative of Ruth. What began as a do-or-die assignment soon transformed into my surprising, interpretive epiphany. I was stunned by Ruth's story and mesmerized by the themes and textures. I gained a profound passion for this biblical story—one to which I have returned numerous times for further research and teaching in subsequent years. When the end-of-semester due date arrived, I submitted a massive stack of discoveries. I had fallen in love with this section of sacred writ. (Just in case you are curious, I *did* pass—with a robust B in the course. Doc Engle proved immensely gracious, further proof of his emotional intelligence.)

Years later, I encountered my second "Gandalf," this time as I was about to begin my doctoral thesis at Denver Seminary. Early in our week of research class, while selecting a "problem" to study (and supposedly solve), I proposed to Dr. David Osborn "something in the vein of helping leaders increase their emotional intelligence." Dr. Osborn had passionately framed the heart of our doctoral program, and our courses carried a thick thread of encouragement for leaders to develop stronger self-awareness and

Afterword & Acknowledgements

personal emotional health. I assumed that he would love my grand idea. Instead, I was stunned to intuit his lack of enthusiasm. His probing questions and cautious nonverbal cues spoke volumes. Though he did not say it, I sensed it. "If you choose that topic, there is a strong likelihood, *you shall not pass!*"

In the following days, my thoughts sparked with the potential for researching ways to help workplace leaders integrate their faith in their daily workplaces, joining God's mission to bless others and bring him glory. To my delight, Doc Osborn gave this idea a great smile of approval! Resourcing workplace leaders toward God's mission became the focus of my doctoral research and eventually my first book, *Henry's Glory: A Story for Discovering Lasting Significance in Your Daily Work.*

As often occurs with compelling ideas, I was not able to shake my sense of the importance of emotional development for leaders. Today, several years removed from those pivotal moments with "Gandalf" Osborn, I am joyfully optimistic about this fusion of theology of work principles and practices, now blended with a theology of emotions and greater spiritual formation. The journey contained in these pages is much more adventuresome and thoughtful because of Doc Osborn's emotional savvy and wise redirection that day "on the bridge." Glancing back into that cavern, I am extremely grateful.

Several additional colorful characters are deserving of my strongest gratitude:

Foremost, my Lord and Savior, Jesus Christ. Thank you for being the most emotionally intelligent leader and most extraordinarily creative worker in the grand story. I am so privileged to follow you on this journey of spiritual formation and emotional development—and oh-so-grateful for your patience with me in the process.

My thoughtful, generous friends and team of leaders at Manor Church. You kindly supplied the space and grace for research and writing, as well as early feedback related to these concepts. These pages became stronger because of your own passion for Christ's work. It's a joy and privilege to serve Christ with you!

Afterword & Acknowledgements

The creative and oh-so-collaborative crew at Wipf and Stock. Your commitment and enthusiasm for working on such people-oriented resources never cease to astound me.

Bill Peel, Ken Eldred, Alex Brubaker, Cheryl Broetje, Christian Overman, David Gill, Randy Kilgore, and a growing team of new friends who are actively engaged in the Faith @ Work conversation. My heart and work are stronger because of your endeavors.

Beth Graves and Kelli Risser. Your gifts and skills in editing, proofreading, and design work are amazing. Thank you for your extra investment of time and pizzazz toward Christ-honoring excellence. Your work made this project so much more compelling.

Mom. It has been an all-out joy to write together. Seeds of this project were actually forty years in the making. When I composed a brief biography of you—"MY MOTHER"—in class as a second grader, you could have scolded me for writing, "My mother does not work. She is a housewife." (Yes indeed, it was a miserably mistaken, male-chauvinistic comment from one clueless kid.) I also reported, "My mother licks black cats. She does not lick snakes." (Of course, I meant to say "like.") Instead of highlighting my typos or scolding me for misguided notions, you chuckled and enthusiastically dubbed it "witty, creative writing." In retrospect, your emotionally-savvy statement was probably a game-changer for my seven-year-old psyche. I have loved to write ever since. It has been an enormous privilege to create this resource together. Immense thanks and love, Mom!

My own (HHP) Gandalf-like event occurred several years ago. I had been spinning many plates for too long. I spent four years working full time while also attending college full time. Added to my busyness were the daily responsibilities of family life and church involvement. After earning my bachelor's degree, I was offered a new position with a local college. The job responsibilities were extremely overwhelming, and the fact that I had to make a two-hour commute each day added to my stress load. Each night, as I fell into bed completely exhausted, I realized I was sacrificing valuable time with my husband, children, grandchildren, and my aging mother. I kept hoping the situation would improve. Alas, it did not improve, and it only became more complicated by the lack of leadership I encountered at work.

Fortunately, the scenario all ended abruptly one cold November day. We were faced with the announcement from the school's administration that the department was being restructured, effective immediately. I was devastated and suddenly began having severe anxiety attacks. A visit to my physician revealed that nothing was physically wrong, but I needed quiet and rest. I was on the brink of a complete emotional breakdown.

My doctor's words immediately spun me into a deep depression and feelings of inadequacy. However, our great God is gracious and kind. The next Sunday, I sat in church under a cloud of darkest gloom. Suddenly, my attention was riveted on the words of our pastor. "If you think you might be having a nervous breakdown, don't worry about it too much. I have had two breakdowns and they aren't all they are cracked up to be." Everyone chuckled, including me. Then he said, "We all strive for mountaintop experiences. But consider this: most of the lush growth occurs in the valleys. Nothing much really grows on top of a mountain. If you are going through a valley experience right now, I guarantee, if you look to the Lord to lead you, it will become a time of growth in your life. Walk though the valley. The Lord will be there to guide and teach you."

I began to heal from that morning forward. My pace slowed. I got a new job that I dearly loved. It was close to home and allowed me the time I so coveted with my family and friends. I learned a great deal during that experience about my own emotional makeup. The Lord taught me that I am not Super Woman. I am his beloved child, and he is all I truly need. I am so thankful that my Savior is so loving and patient with this stubborn child. He always understands my emotions and has been there to lead me through every one of life's darkest valleys.

I am also very thankful for my fantastic friends, pastors, and coworkers. The Lord has wonderfully enriched my life with these individuals. Many faithful pastors have patiently helped direct my paths. The Lord has blessed me with close friends who have always listened to me through both good times and difficult times. Across the years, God has brought faithful coworkers into my life, colleagues who have led wisely and consistently encouraged me to climb to higher ground.

I am blessed with such a wonderful family. They have always been there to support me in my lowest moments and to applaud me during my mountaintop events. My mother gave me a rich appreciation for God's beautiful Word. She read and discussed the Bible at breakfast and bedtime when we were children. Mom taught me to pray. My own dear children, John and Betsy, are one of my greatest joys in this life. It is an honor to be called "Mom" by them. I love you guys very much. I was overwhelmed when John asked his old mom to share her thoughts and experiences in this book. Thank you, Son! May God always use your gifts for his glory.

About the Authors

Holly Hall-Pletcher was born in Batavia, New York in 1949. She grew up in a small town in Ohio and enjoyed an idyllic childhood. Her mother was the quintessential 1950s homemaker, and her father was the typical, white-shirt-and-tie, hardworking dad. Holly married her high school sweetheart, Ken Pletcher, in 1968. They had two children, John and Betsy. While completing educational endeavors and serving in various areas of ministry, the Pletcher family lived in several different states. Even when the children were young, Ken and Holly included their children in every part of ministry. Serving the Lord together was always a joyful part of family life.

Holly holds a Master of Arts in Adult Education from the University of Phoenix and a Bachelor of Science in English from the Ohio State University. Her hobbies include reading, sewing, and knitting. She recently retired and enjoys spending time with family.

John Elton Pletcher is crazy about connecting with people over delicious coffee. He also enjoys running, watching movies, reading, playing baseball with his boys, and taking long walks with his golden retriever, Brodimus Maximus.

John serves as lead pastor at Manor Church in Lancaster, Pennsylvania and also teaches as adjunct faculty at Eastern University and Evangelical Seminary. He is married to Nancy, and they have three sons, Jarod, Joel and Josiah.

Pletch, as friends call him, holds the Doctor of Ministry in Leadership from Denver Seminary and the Master of Divinity from Baptist Bible Seminary (PA).

About the Authors

John's book, *Henry's Glory: A Story for Discovering Lasting Significance in Your Daily Work*, is available through wipfandstock.com.

Passionate about helping leaders develop bigger hearts and skills for missional living, he is available for consultation, coaching, storytelling, and conference/seminar speaking during a limited number of days each year.

For further information about scheduling John for your event, plus reading his engaging blog and other creative resources, visit johneltonpletcher.com.

Bibliography

Berlin, Adele. *Poetics and Interpretation of Biblical Narrative*. Winona Lake, IN: Eisenbrauns, 1994.
Block, Douglas. *Healing from Depression: 12 Weeks to a Better Mood*. Berkley: Celestial Arts, 2002.
Broetje, Ralph. http://www.firstfruits.com/company-history.html.
Brown, Brené. *Daring Greatly: How the Courage to Be Vulnerable Transforms the Way We Live, Love, Parent, and Lead*. New York: Avery, 2012.
Brown, Kristin. "Why We Can—and Should—Grieve at Work." http://blog.tifwe.org/why-we-can-and-should-grieve-at-work/.
Burton, Neel. *Heaven and Hell: The Psychology of the Emotions*. Exeter, Devon UK: Acheron, 2015.
Carter, Les, and Frank Minrith. *The Freedom From Depression Workbook*. Nashville: Thomas Nelson, 1995.
Catton, Bruce. *Terrible Swift Sword*. Garden City, New York: Doubleday, 1963.
Churchill, Winston. *My Early Life: 1874–1904, With a New Introduction by William Manchester*. New York: Simon and Schuster, 1996.
Clarke, Alison J. *Tupperware: The Promise of Plastic in 1950s America*. Washington: Smithsonian Institution, 1999.
Cloud, Henry. *9 Things You Simply Must Do to Succeed in Love and Life*. Nashville: Integrity, 2004.
Comer, John Mark. *Loveology: God. Love. Marriage. Sex. And the never-ending story of male and female*. Grand Rapids: Zondervan, 2013.
Darwin, Charles. *The Expression of the Emotions in Man and Animals*. London: John Murray, 1872.
Dillard, Raymond B., and Tremper Longman III. *An Introduction to the Old Testament*. Grand Rapids: Zondervan, 1994.
Ekman, Paul, et al. "Pan-cultural Elements in Facial Displays of Emotion," *Science, 164*.
Fentress-Williams, Judy. *Ruth*. Abingdon Old Testament Commentaries. Nashville: Abingdon, 2012.
Fikkert, Brian, and Russell Mask. *From Dependence to Dignity: How to Alleviate Poverty through Church-Centered Microfinance*. Grand Rapids: Zondervan, 2015.

Bibliography

Flood, Charles Bracelen. *Grant and Sherman: The Friendship that Won the Civil War*. New York: Farrar, Straus and Giroux, 2005.

Goleman, Daniel. *Emotional Intelligence: Why It Can Matter More than IQ*. New York: Bantam, 1995.

———. *Primal Leadership: Learning to Lead with Emotional Intelligence*. Boston: Harvard Business School Press, 2004.

Grudem, Wayne. "How Business in Itself Can Glorify God." In *On Kingdom Business: Transforming Missions Through Entrepreneurial Strategies*, edited by Tetsunao Yamamori and Kenneth A. Eldred, 127–51. Wheaton: Crossway, 2003.

Hamlin, E. John. *Ruth: Surely There Is a Future*. International Theological Commentary. Grand Rapids: Wm. B. Eerdmans, 1996.

Hunter, James Davison. *To Change the World: The Irony, Tragedy, and Possibility of Christianity in the Late Modern World*. New York: Oxford University Press, 2010.

James, Carolyn Custis. *The Gospel of Ruth: Loving God Enough to Break the Rules*. Grand Rapids: Zondervan, 2008.

Johnston, Elizabeth, and Leah Olson. *The Feeling Brain: The Biology and Psychology of Emotions*. New York: W.W. Norton and Company, 2015.

Kealing, Bob. *Tupperware Unsealed: Brownie Wise, Earl Tupper, and the Home Party Pioneers*. Gainesville: University Press of Florida, 2008.

King, Tim, and Frank Martin. *Furious Pursuit: Why God Will Never Let You Go*. Colorado Springs: Waterbrook, 2006.

LeDoux, Joseph. *The Emotional Brain: The Mysterious Underpinnings of the Emotional Life*. New York: Simon and Schuster, 1996.

———. "The Amygdala." *Current Biology*, 17, R8868–R8874.

Lendino, Jamie. "The History of the Car Stereo," http://www.pcmag.com/article2/0,2817,2399878,00.asp.

Linafelt, Tod. *Ruth*. Berit Olam: Studies in Hebrew Narrative and Poetry, edited by David W. Cotter. Collegeville, MN: The Liturgical, 1999.

Mulholland, M. Robert Jr. *Invitation to A Journey: A Road Map for Spiritual Formation*. Downers Grove: Intervarsity, 1993.

Muncaster, Ralph O. *Why Does God Allow Suffering?* Examine the Evidence. Eugene, OR: Harvest House, 2001.

Nelson, Tom. *Work Matters: Connecting Sunday Worship to Monday Work*. Wheaton: Crossway, 2011.

Palmer, Robert C., and Heather Palmer Welesko. *The Diamond of Adversity: A Theology of Suffering*. Minneapolis: Next Step Resources, 2014.

Peel, Bill, and Walt Larimore. *Workplace Grace: Becoming a Spiritual Influence at Work*. Longview, TX: LeTourneau, 2014.

Peterson, Eugene H. *A Long Obedience in the Same Direction: Discipleship in an Instant Society*. Downers Grove: InterVarsity, 2000.

Sakenfeld, Katharine Doob. *Ruth*. Interpretation: A Bible Commentary for Teaching and Preaching, edited by James Luther Mays. Louisville: John Knox, 1999.

Bibliography

Sasson, Jack M. *Ruth: A New Translation with a Philological Commentary and a Formalist-Folklorist Interpretation, 2nd Edition.* Sheffield: Sheffield Academic, 1995.

Scazerro, Peter. *The Emotionally Healthy Leader: How Transforming Your Inner Life Will Deeply Transform Your Church, Team, and the World.* Grand Rapids: Zondervan, 2015.

Schaap, Jeremy. *Cinderella Man. James J. Braddock, Max Baer, and the Greatest Upset in Boxing History.* New York: Houghton Mifflin, 2005.

Schelske, Marc Alan. "5 Things You Learned About Emotion in Church That Aren't True." http://marcalanschelske.com/5-things-you-learned-about-emotion-in-church-that-arent-true/.

Seamands, David A. *Healing for Damaged Emotions: Recovering from the Memories That Cause Our Pain.* Wheaton: Victor, 1981.

Stanley, Andy. *The New Rules for Love, Sex, and Dating.* Grand Rapids: Zondervan, 2014.

Stevens, R. Paul, and Alvin Ung. *Taking Your Soul to Work: Overcoming the Nine Deadly Sins of the Workplace.* Grand Rapids: William B. Eerdmans, 2010.

Storr, Anthony. *Churchill's Black Dog, Kafka's Mice and Other Phenomena of the Human Mind.* New York: Ballantine, 1988.

Swindoll, Charles. *Insight for Living Daily Podcast: Traveling a Rough and Rugged Road Part 2,* aired July 23, 2015.

Theology of Work Project, *Theology of Work Bible Commentary,* ed. William Messenger. http://www.theologyofwork.org/old-testament/ruth-and-work.

Tornfelt, John. *Reunion: Meeting Ourselves Again for the First Time.* North Charleston: CreateSpace, 2012.

Tupperware: About the Film Biography: Earl Silas Tupper, http://www.pbs.org/wgbh/americanexperience/features/biograpy/tupperware-tupper/.

Van Duzer, Jeff. *Why Business Matters to God: (And What Still Needs to Be Fixed).* Downers Grove, IL: InterVarsity, 2010.

Wright, Christopher J.H. *The Mission of God: Unlocking the Bible's Grand Narrative.* Downers Grove, IL: InterVarsity, 2006.

Wright, H. Norman. *Helping Those Who Hurt: How To Be There for Your Friends In Need.* Minneapolis: Bethany, 2003.

www.ingramcontent.com/pod-product-compliance
Lightning Source LLC
Chambersburg PA
CBHW071502150426
43191CB00009B/1405